# Contents

Introduction ................... 3

## Unit 1: Teacher Resources
Newsletter ..................... 4
Border Page .................... 5
Special Days in November ....... 6
November Calendar .............. 7
Calendar Activities ............ 8
Special Days Teacher Information ... 8
National Sandwich Day Activity Master ... 9
The Pilgrims' First Year Activity Master ... 10

## Unit 2: Thankful for Thanksgiving
Teacher Information ............ 11
Arts and Crafts ................ 12
Kid's Kitchen .................. 13
Poem and Book List ............. 14
Bulletin Board ................. 15
Centers
    Language Center ............ 16
    Math Center ................ 16
    Science Center ............. 17
    Social Studies Center ...... 17
    Writing Center ............. 18
    Game Center ................ 18
    Physical Development Skills Center ... 19
    Communication Center ....... 19
Patterns, Cards, and Activity Masters
    Pilgrim Puppet Patterns .... 20
    Turkey and Feathers Patterns ... 21
    Complete Turkey Patterns ... 22
    Turkey Parts Patterns ...... 22
    Game Cube Pattern .......... 24
    Food Picture Cards ......... 25

## Unit 3: Knowing Native Americans
Teacher Information ............ 26
Arts and Crafts ................ 27
Kid's Kitchen .................. 28
Poem and Book List ............. 29
Bulletin Board ................. 30
Centers
    Language Center ............ 31
    Math Center ................ 31
    Science Center ............. 32
    Social Studies Center ...... 32
    Writing Center ............. 33
    Art Center ................. 33
    Communication Center ....... 34
    Game Center ................ 34
Patterns, Poster, and Activity Masters
    Symbol Patterns Poster ..... 35
    Plank House Pattern ........ 36
    ABC Order Activity Master .. 37
    Basket and Fish Patterns ... 38
    Native American Homes Activity Master ... 39
    A Clan for Me Activity Master ... 40

## Unit 4: Magnificent Mammals
Teacher Information ............ 41
Arts and Crafts ................ 42
Kid's Kitchen .................. 43
Rap and Book List .............. 44
Bulletin Board ................. 45
Centers
    Language Center ............ 46
    Math Center ................ 46
    Science Center ............. 47
    Social Studies Center ...... 47
    Writing Center ............. 48
    Art Center ................. 48
    Literacy Center ............ 49
    Technology Center .......... 49
Cards and Activity Masters
    Mammal Picture Cards ....... 50
    Zoo Time Treasure Activity Master ... 52
    Hairy Facts Activity Master ... 53
    Feeding on the Farm Activity Master ... 54
    Mammal Opposites Activity Master ... 55

## Unit 5: Take a Vote
Teacher Information . . . . . . . . . . . . . . . . . 56
Arts and Crafts . . . . . . . . . . . . . . . . . . . . . 57
Kid's Kitchen . . . . . . . . . . . . . . . . . . . . . . 58
Chant and Book List . . . . . . . . . . . . . . . . 59
Bulletin Board . . . . . . . . . . . . . . . . . . . . . 60
Centers
    Language Center . . . . . . . . . . . . . . . . 61
    Math Center . . . . . . . . . . . . . . . . . . . 61
    Science Center . . . . . . . . . . . . . . . . . 62
    Social Studies Center . . . . . . . . . . . . . 62
    Writing Center . . . . . . . . . . . . . . . . . 63
    Art Center . . . . . . . . . . . . . . . . . . . . . 63
    Technology Center . . . . . . . . . . . . . . 64
    Communication Center . . . . . . . . . . . 64
Patterns and Activity Masters
    Who Will You Vote For?
        Activity Master . . . . . . . . . . . . . . . 65
    Super Dog and Great Cat Patterns . . . 66
    The Sounds of g and s
        Activity Master . . . . . . . . . . . . . . . 67
    Ballots and Boxes Patterns . . . . . . . . . 68
    Sharing the News Activity Master . . . 69
    Ballot Patterns . . . . . . . . . . . . . . . . . 70

## Unit 6: Food and You
Teacher Information . . . . . . . . . . . . . . . . . 71
Arts and Crafts . . . . . . . . . . . . . . . . . . . . . 72
Kid's Kitchen . . . . . . . . . . . . . . . . . . . . . . 73
Choral Poem and Book List . . . . . . . . . . . 74
Bulletin Board . . . . . . . . . . . . . . . . . . . . . 75
Centers
    Language Center . . . . . . . . . . . . . . . . 76
    Math Center . . . . . . . . . . . . . . . . . . . 76
    Science Center . . . . . . . . . . . . . . . . . 77
    Social Studies Center . . . . . . . . . . . . . 77
    Writing Center . . . . . . . . . . . . . . . . . 78
    Communication Center . . . . . . . . . . . 78
    Game Center . . . . . . . . . . . . . . . . . . . 79
    Physical Development Skills Center . . . 79

Cards and Activity Masters
    Time to Eat Activity Master . . . . . . . . 80
    Food Graph Activity Master . . . . . . . . 81
    Food Picture Cards . . . . . . . . . . . . . . 82
    My Favorite Food Activity Master . . . . 84
    The Path to Good Health
        Activity Master . . . . . . . . . . . . . . . 85

## Unit 7: Author Study— Marc Brown
Teacher Information . . . . . . . . . . . . . . . . . 86
Literature Selection and Activities . . . . . . . 87
Book List . . . . . . . . . . . . . . . . . . . . . . . . . 88
Patterns and Activity Masters
    Bookmark Patterns . . . . . . . . . . . . . . 89
    Play a Turkey Activity Master . . . . . . . 90
    Arthur's Play Activity Master . . . . . . . 91

## Center Icons Patterns . . . . . . . . 92

## Student Awards Patterns . . . . . . 95

## Student Award/Calendar Day Patterns . . . . . . . . . . . . . . . . 96

# Introduction

This series of monthly activity books is designed to give first and second grade teachers a collection of hands-on activities and ideas for each month of the year. The activities are standards-based and reflect the philosophy that children have different styles of learning. The teacher can use these ideas to enhance the development of the core subjects of language, math, social studies, and science, as well as the social/emotional and physical growth of children. Moreover, the opportunity to promote reading skills is present throughout the series and should be incorporated whenever possible.

## Organization and Features

Each book consists of seven units:

**Unit 1** provides reproducible pages and information for the month in general.
- a newsletter outline to promote parent communication
- a blank thematic border page
- a list of special days in the month
- calendar ideas to promote special holidays
- a blank calendar grid that can also be used as an incentive chart

**Units 2–6** include an array of activities for five **theme** topics. Each unit includes
- teacher information on the theme
- arts and crafts ideas
- a food activity
- poetry, language skills (songs, poems, raps, and chants), and books
- bulletin board ideas
- center activities correlated to specific learning standards (Language arts, math, science, social studies, and writing are included in each theme.)

Implement the activities in a way that best meets the needs of individual children.

**Unit 7** focuses on a well-known **children's author**. The unit includes
- a biography of the author
- activities based on a literature selection
- a list of books by the author
- reproducible bookmarks

In addition, each book contains
- reproducible **icons** suitable to use as labels for centers in the classroom. The icons coordinate with the centers in the book. They may also be used with a work assignment chart to aid in assigning children to centers.
- reproducible **student awards**
- **calendar day pattern** with suggested activities

## Research Base

Howard Gardner's theory of multiple intelligences, or learning styles, validates teaching thematically and using a variety of approaches to help children learn. Providing a variety of experiences will assure that each child has an opportunity to learn in a comfortable way.

Following are the learning styles identified by Howard Gardner.
- **Verbal/Linguistic** learners need opportunities to read, listen, write, learn new words, and tell stories.
- **Bodily/Kinesthetic** learners learn best through physical activities.
- **Musical** learners enjoy music activities.
- **Logical/Mathematical** learners need opportunities to problem solve, count, measure, and do patterning activities.
- **Visual/Spatial** learners need opportunities to paint, draw, sculpt, and create artworks.
- **Interpersonal** learners benefit from group discussions and group projects.
- **Intrapersonal** learners learn best in solitary activities, such as reading, writing in journals, and reflecting on information.
- **Naturalist** learners need opportunities to observe weather and nature and to take care of animals and plants.
- **Existential** learners can be fostered in the early years by asking children to think and respond, by discussions, and by writing.

Gardner, H. (1994). *Frames of mind.* New York: Basic Books.

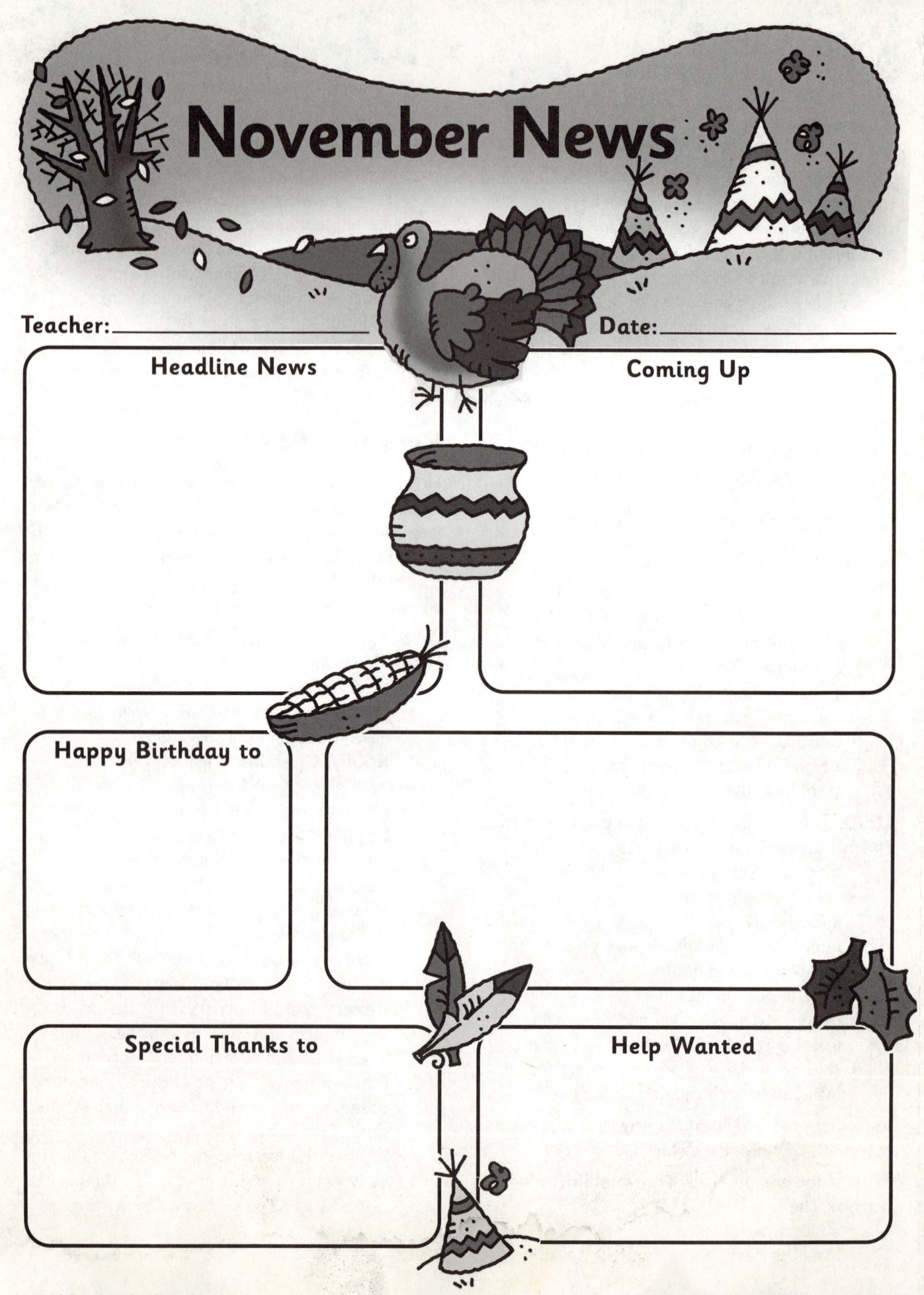

# November News

Teacher:_____  Date:_____

**Headline News**

**Coming Up**

**Happy Birthday to**

**Special Thanks to**

**Help Wanted**

# November

# Special Days in November

**National American Indian Heritage Month** Have children celebrate with activities from the Knowing Native Americans unit that begins on page 26.

**National Peanut Butter Lovers Month** Have children shell peanuts. Then grind the peanuts in a food processor with a small amount of oil and salt. Enjoy a snack of peanut butter and crackers.

**1 National Author's Day** Honor an author today. Display books written by a popular children's author in the reading center. Select a book to read aloud.

**3 Sandwich Day** Have children dictate a sentence telling what they would put on a favorite sandwich and have them draw a picture of it.

**5 National Donut Day** Cut a hole in a biscuit with a donut cutter. Deep-fry the donuts and have children roll them in cinnamon and sugar when cooled. Serve to children as a snack.

**7 Hug a Bear Day** Have children bring a favorite stuffed bear to class and read a bear story aloud to them.

**8 X-Ray Day (day the X-ray was discovered)** Display an X-ray and discuss the different shapes of bones.

**10 Sesame Street debuted in 1969** Display several books about Sesame Street characters. Have children draw a picture of their favorite Sesame Street friend.

**11 Veterans Day** Invite a veteran or a member of the armed forces to speak with children about his or her job. Before or after the speech, discuss the meaning of freedom and how other people have served the United States to help us remain free.

**16 Button Day** Display a container of buttons and have children sort them by various attributes or use them to make patterns.

**17 Take a Hike Day** Take a walk around the school grounds and make a list of what children see on the walk.

**20 National Children's Day** Ask children to tell what they like most about being a child and record their answers.

**21 World Hello Day** Have children say hello to ten people during the day.

**25 Marc Brown's Birthday** Read a book written by Marc Brown in honor of his birthday.

**26 Charles Schulz's Birthday (1922)** Display a picture of Snoopy. Have children tell what they know about the character. Encourage them to watch "A Charlie Brown Thanksgiving" when it airs on television.

# November

| Sunday | Monday | Tuesday | Wednesday | Thursday | Friday | Saturday |
|---|---|---|---|---|---|---|
| | | | | | | |
| | | | | | | |
| | | | | | | |
| | | | | | | |
| | | | | | | |

# Using the Calendar for Basic Instruction in the Classroom

The children you teach may enjoy using the calendar-related games and activities on this page to practice other skills.

**Word Problems** During daily calendar time, practice problem solving by asking children to use the calendar to answer a question. For example: It rained all week except on Monday, Wednesday, and Thursday. On which days did it rain? You may wish to relate the questions to holidays or units of study.

**Graphing** Make a line graph to hang on the wall. Write the numbers 1–6 on the vertical axis and the twelve months of the year on the horizontal axis. Find out how many children have a birthday in each month and record on the graph. Connect the points to finish the line graph. You may wish to have the children copy the data and make individual line graphs.

**Patterning** Give children a calendar page for any month that you choose. Decide on a specific color pattern, such as red, yellow, and green. Have children color three days in the middle of the calendar red, yellow, and green. Then, have them color all of the remaining days using the same pattern. They will be extending patterns forward and backward.

**Math Facts** Have children play a calendar toss game. Make a large calendar page on a plastic tablecloth and lay it on the floor. Select a number that the children need to practice with addition, subtraction, multiplication, or division facts, for example, subtracting the number 9. Give players one beanbag each and have children take turns tossing the beanbag on the calendar. Each player will subtract the number 9 from the number that the beanbag lands on. You may wish to have them write the equation.

**Special Days** You may wish to use the activity masters on pages 9 and 10 to expand children's knowledge of favorite holidays and special days. The information for these special days is included below.

**National Sandwich Day** honors the creation of the first sandwich by the English nobleman, John Montagu, the fourth Earl of Sandwich. While playing a game, Earl Montagu got hungry. He asked a servant to put some meat between two slices of bread. It became an instant success. Nearly 45 billion sandwiches are eaten by Americans each year. It is appropriate that this popular food is given special recognition on the Earl of Sandwich's birthday, November 3.

**Thanksgiving Day** celebrates the Pilgrim feast of 1621. The Native Americans had shown the Pilgrims how to plant seeds, and because of their help, the Pilgrims had a good harvest. They invited the Native Americans to a three-day feast, which is known as the first Thanksgiving. However, the colonists didn't repeat it again. In 1789, George Washington proclaimed November 26 as a public day of thanksgiving and prayer. President Abraham Lincoln later proclaimed the last Thursday in November as Thanksgiving Day. Finally, in 1939, President Franklin Roosevelt changed the date to the fourth Thursday in November in an effort to give store merchants more time to sell for the Christmas season. Congress made the date permanent soon after.

Name _____   Date _____

# National Sandwich Day

**Directions:** Read the story.

A long time ago, an English lord was playing a game. He got hungry. He asked someone to bring him food. He wanted some meat between two pieces of bread. Now the man could hold the food in one hand and still play the game with the other hand. He liked the food. It was very good.

We eat this food today. Do you know what it is called? A sandwich! The food was named for the man who thought of it. The man's name was the Earl of Sandwich. Some people decided to honor the sandwich on November 3. It is the same day as the birthday of the Earl of Sandwich!

**Directions:** Draw a picture of your favorite sandwich.

Name _____  Date _____

# The Pilgrims' First Year

**Directions:** Read the chart below. Then answer the questions.

| Date | During the First Year |
| --- | --- |
| November 1620 | People on the *Mayflower* saw land. |
| December 1620 | The *Mayflower* landed at Plymouth. |
| March 1621 | The Pilgrims met Samoset. |
| April 1621 | The *Mayflower* went back to England. |
| October 1621 | The Pilgrims harvested food. |
| November 1621 | The Pilgrims celebrated with Native Americans. |

1. What month and year did the *Mayflower* land at Plymouth?

2. What happened first in 1621?

3. What month and year did the *Mayflower* leave Plymouth?

4. What happened last in 1621?

# Giving Thanks for Facts

The *Mayflower* sailed from England on September 16, 1620, with 102 passengers who were in search of religious freedom.

The journey was made difficult by the poor living conditions and scarcity of food on the ship.

Land was sighted on November 11, after 65 days at sea. The ship dropped anchor on November 21 near what is today Provincetown, Massachusetts.

On that day, the men signed the *Mayflower Compact* as a temporary form of government. That document would maintain their loyalty to the king of England and set their own laws.

After several weeks, the Pilgrims decided to settle in the area that is now known as Plymouth Rock. They landed in the area on December 21.

Because of the harsh weather, the Pilgrims lived on the *Mayflower* through the winter months, while clearing fields and building houses. Diseases spread, and half of the colonists died.

The Pilgrims first met a Native American named Samoset in March of 1621. He then introduced them to Squanto, who could speak English. Squanto showed the Pilgrims how to tap maple trees for sap, how to hunt and fish, and how best to plant seeds. This included fertilizing the corn seeds by burying dead fish below the seeds.

The harvest of 1621 was bountiful. Sometime in mid-October, the Pilgrim Governor William Bradford declared a day of thanksgiving to be shared by all the colonists and the neighboring Native Americans.

Chief Massasoit and ninety men from the Wamponoag tribe came to joined the 41 Pilgrim men. The celebration lasted three days. They played games, ran races, marched, played drums, and demonstrated their bow and arrow and musket skills.

No women from the tribe attended the celebration. Only four Pilgrim women had survived the first winter. According to custom, they were responsible for the meal preparation and were not invited.

# Paper Plate Mayflower

## Materials

- small paper plates
- craft sticks
- white construction paper
- brown markers or crayons
- glue
- ruler or measuring tape
- scissors

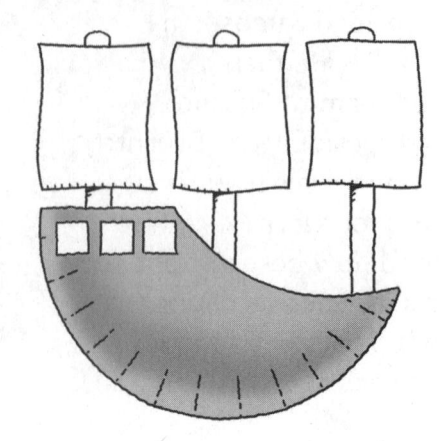

## Directions

**Teacher Preparation:** Cut the white construction paper into three-inch strips. Cut the paper plates in half. Each child will need a strip of paper, half of a paper plate, and three craft sticks.

1. Cut out a section of a paper plate so it slopes like the front of the *Mayflower*.
2. Draw three small squares on the uncut part of the plate for ship windows.
3. Color the plate brown, but leave the windows white.
4. Cut a paper strip into three pieces to make sails.
5. Glue each paper sail on a craft stick.
6. Glue the sticks on the back of the paper plate ship.

# Pilgrim Puppets

## Materials

- patterns on page 20
- small lunch bags
- recycled file folders
- yarn (in hair colors)
- white and black construction paper
- markers or crayons
- scissors
- glue

## Directions

**Teacher Preparation:** Duplicate and cut out the hats and collar patterns. Trace several patterns on the folders to make templates and cut them out. Cut the white and black paper into rectangles close in size to the patterns for children. Provide each child with a bag, templates, and construction paper.

1. Trace a Pilgrim hat and collar. Cut them out.
2. Draw a face on the bottom of the bag.
3. Color the rest of the bag black for the clothes.
4. Cut yarn to make the hair. Glue it around the face.
5. Glue the hat and collar on the puppet.

# Pumpkin Pie Cups

## You will need
- canned pumpkin
- whipped topping
- crushed graham crackers
- cinnamon
- plastic cups
- plastic spoons
- bowls
- measuring cups

## Directions
1. Sprinkle the crushed graham crackers in the bottom of a cup.
2. In a bowl, mix ½ cup of pumpkin with ¼ cup of whipped topping.
3. Spoon the mixture over the graham crackers.
4. Place a spoonful of whipped topping on the mixture.
5. Sprinkle cinnamon lightly on top.

**Note:** Be aware of children who may have food allergies.

# Thanksgiving Day

People think of Pilgrims
 when Thanksgiving Day is near.
The Pilgrims sailed away from home
 and lived in danger for a year.
With the help of Squanto,
 who became a special friend,
The Pilgrims had much food to eat
 right after summer's end.
So they asked their helpful friends,
 who lived with them in peace,
To come and celebrate with them
 for a three-day feast.
Now since the first Thanksgiving
 was so joyous and such fun,
Don't you think that we should have
 three days instead of one?

## Thankful for Good Books . . .

**How Many Days to America?: A Thanksgiving Story**
by Eve Bunting (Houghton Mifflin)

**If You Sailed on the Mayflower**
by Ann McGovern (Scholastic)

**If You Were at the First Thanksgiving**
by Anne Kamma (Scholastic)

**I Know an Old Lady Who Swallowed a Pie**
by Alison Jackson (Puffin)

**It's Thanksgiving**
by Jack Prelutsky
(William Morrow & Company)

**The Night Before Thanksgiving**
by Natasha Wing (Grossset & Dunlap)

**The Pilgrim's First Thanksgiving**
by Ann McGovern (Scholastic)

**Samuel Eaton's Day: A Day in the Life of a Pilgrim Boy**
by Kate Waters (Scholastic)

**Sarah Morton's Day: A Day in the Life of a Pilgrim Girl**
by Kate Waters (Scholastic)

**Squanto and the Miracle of Thanksgiving**
by Eric Metaxas (Thomas Nelson)

**Tapenum's Day: A Wampanoag Indian Boy in Pilgrim Times**
by Kate Waters (Scholastic)

**Thanksgiving in the White House**
by Gary Hines (Holt, Henry Books)

## Thanksgiving Riddle
### Why do turkeys "gobble, gobble"?

**They never learned good table manners!**

## Materials

- white and green construction paper
- craft paper
- border
- brown, red, yellow, green, and orange tempera paint
- markers
- paintbrushes
- paint containers
- scissors
- stapler
- glue

## Directions

**Teacher Preparation:** Cover the bulletin board with craft paper. Add a border. Write or cut out the letters for the riddle and staple them to the bulletin board. Cut the green paper into one-inch strips. Prepare a paint center.

## Riddle

Why do turkeys "gobble, gobble"?
They never learned good table manners!

1. Brush brown paint on the palm and thumb to make the turkey's body.
2. Brush each finger with red, yellow, green, or orange paint to make the tail feathers.
3. Press the hand in the center of the white construction paper. Set it aside to dry.
4. Fringe cut a green paper strip to make grass. Glue it to the bottom of the white paper.
5. Draw and color an eye, a beak, a wattle, and feet with markers.

Help children staple their turkeys on the bulletin board. Lead children in a discussion about good table manners.

# Thanksgiving Centers

## Language Center

**Language Arts Standard**
Recognizes syllables in words

### Turkey Syllables

**Materials**
- patterns on page 21
- scissors
- marker
- brown, red, yellow, green, and orange construction paper

**Teacher Preparation:** Duplicate several turkeys on brown paper and the feathers on yellow, red, green, and orange paper. Cut them out. Write spelling words, holiday words, or other content words that children may be learning on the turkey bodies.

Help children read each word. Then have them add feathers to the turkey's body to show the number of syllables.

## Math Center

**Math Standard**
Counts by twos, fives, and tens

### Skip-Count Turkey

**Materials**
- patterns on page 22
- white construction paper
- scissors
- laminate
- water-filled spray bottle
- 5 file folders
- markers
- glue
- washable markers
- paper towels

**Teacher Preparation:** Duplicate, cut out, and color 50 turkeys. Glue five turkeys in two rows on each file folder. Then laminate the folders.

Using one folder, invite children to count the turkeys' feet by twos and write the numbers near the feet. Using two folders, ask them to count the feathers by fives and write those numbers near the feathers. Finally, challenge children to count the turkeys on the five folders by tens and write those numbers on the tabs.

# Thanksgiving Centers

### Science Center

**Science Standard**
Identifies characteristics of organisms

## Name That Turkey

### Materials

- patterns on pages 22 and 23
- felt board
- scissors
- glue
- brown, yellow, and red felt
- construction paper
- marker

**Teacher Preparation:** Trace a turkey body, head, wing, and five feathers on brown felt. Trace a foot, eye, and beak on yellow felt. Trace the wattle on red felt. Cut out all the pieces. Write a label for each body part on construction paper cards. Glue squares of felt on the backs of cards.

Help children read the names of the body parts. Then challenge them to make a turkey on the felt board using the felt pieces. Have them label the parts with the cards.

### Social Studies Center

**Social Studies Standard**
Recognizes important historical figures

## Squanto Helps

### Materials

- *Squanto and the Miracle of Thanksgiving* by Eric Metaxas
- dried corn
- brown and gray construction paper
- scissors
- glue

Read aloud the book. Remind children that Squanto taught the Pilgrims how to put a fish in the ground with the seeds to help the plants grow strong and healthy. Then invite children to cut a piece of brown paper into a dirt-mound shape. Have them draw a fish on gray paper, cut it out, and glue it to the paper mound. Finally, have them glue four pieces of corn above the fish.

# Thanksgiving Centers

## Writing Center

**Language Arts Standard**
Understands that written words are separated by spaces

### Thankful Writing

**Materials**
- drawing paper
- crayons

Discuss with children the things that Pilgrims were thankful for on the first Thanksgiving. Be sure that children include health, houses, and their Native American friends. Then invite children to write a sentence telling what they are thankful for. Encourage them to draw a picture to go along with their sentences.

## Game Center

**Social Studies Standard**
Understands how people lived long ago

### Pilgrim Food Fun

**Materials**

pattern on page 24, picture cards on page 25, white construction paper, tape, markers, scissors

**Teacher Preparation:** Duplicate the cube pattern on white paper, color the pictures, and cut out the figure. Form the cube and tape it closed. Add tape along the sides of the cube to make it sturdy. Duplicate a set of cards for each child.

Have children color and cut out the food pictures. Explain to children that the Pilgrims grew, gathered, and hunted their food. Help children name the foods and sort them into the appropriate categories: growing, gathering, hunting. Next, point out the symbols on the cube and talk about what they represent. A hoe represents growing. A basket represents gathering. A musket represents hunting. Then invite children to play a game. Have them roll the cube, identify the category, and select a card showing the food in that category. The object is to select each food card. Players who roll one category, but already have all the foods, skip that turn. The first player to get all nine cards says "Pilgrim" and is the winner.

**Note:** You may wish to have children fold a sheet of paper and staple two sides together to form an envelope to store the cards.

# Thanksgiving Centers

### Physical Development Skills Center

**Physical Education Standard**
Lifts and supports his/her own weight in selected activities that develop muscular strength and endurance of the arms, shoulders, abdomen, back, and legs such as hanging, hopping, and jumping

## Jump to Plymouth Rock

**Materials**
- blue, gray, and brown felt
- scissors

**Teacher Preparation:** Cut out a *Mayflower* shape from the brown felt. Cut out a rock shape from the gray felt. Cut a large blue square for ocean water. Place the ocean water felt on the floor and lay the rock on one side. Lay the *Mayflower* on the water next to the rock.

Remind children that the Pilgrims decided to start their colony in what is now Plymouth, Massachusetts. Legend says that they stepped on Plymouth Rock to get to shore. Invite children to role-play Pilgrims. Have them step from the ship to the rock. After children have completed the task, repeatedly move the ship away from the rock so that children are jumping increased distances safely.

### Communication Center

**Social Studies Standard**
Identifies customs associated with holidays

## My Family Thanksgiving

**Materials**
- drawing paper
- crayons

Ask children to draw a picture of their favorite part of Thanksgiving. Encourage them to write a caption. Then have small groups of children meet to discuss their pictures and holiday traditions.

# Pilgrim Puppet Patterns

Use with "Pilgrim Puppets" on page 12.

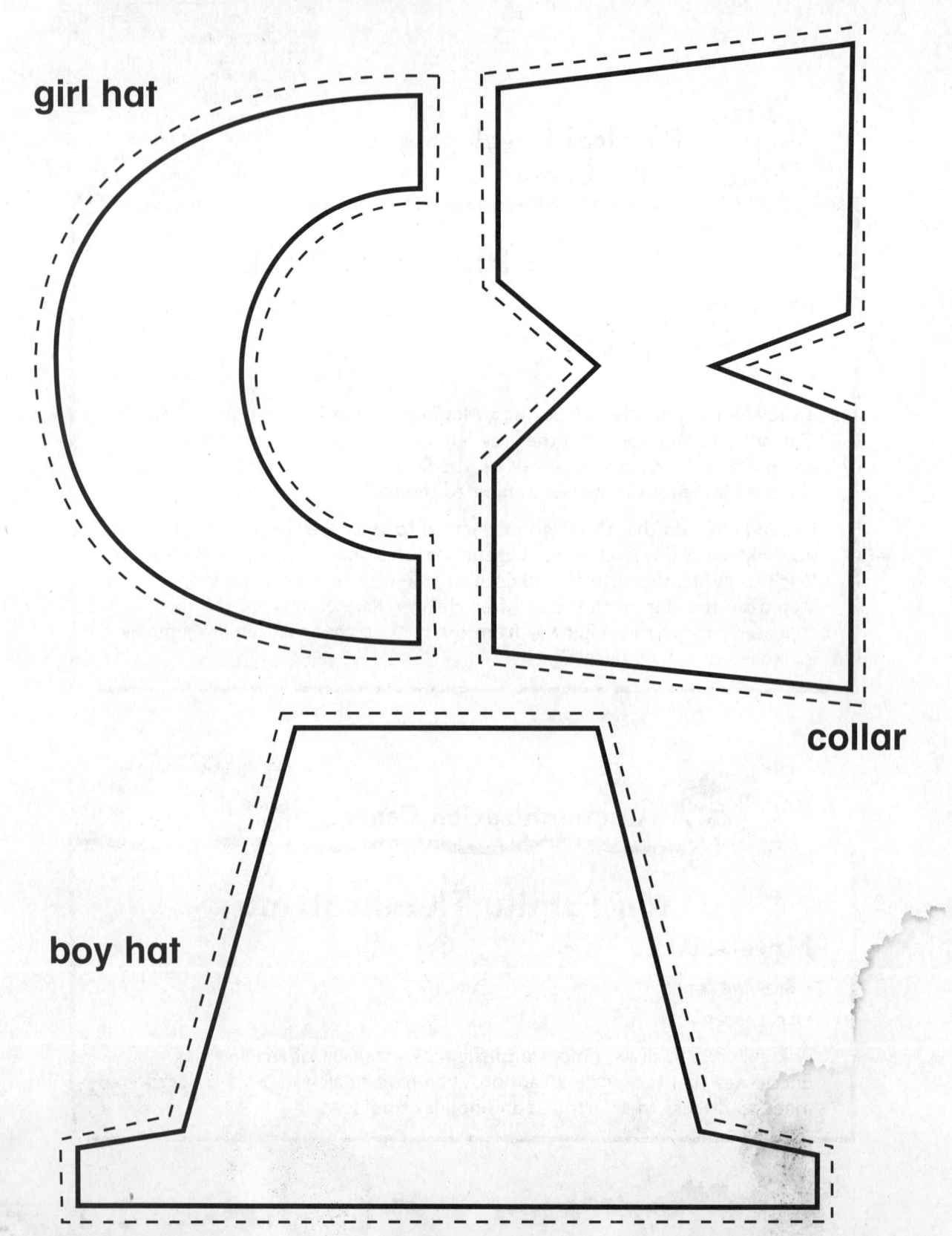

girl hat

collar

boy hat

# Turkey and Feathers Patterns

Use with "Turkey Syllables" on page 16.

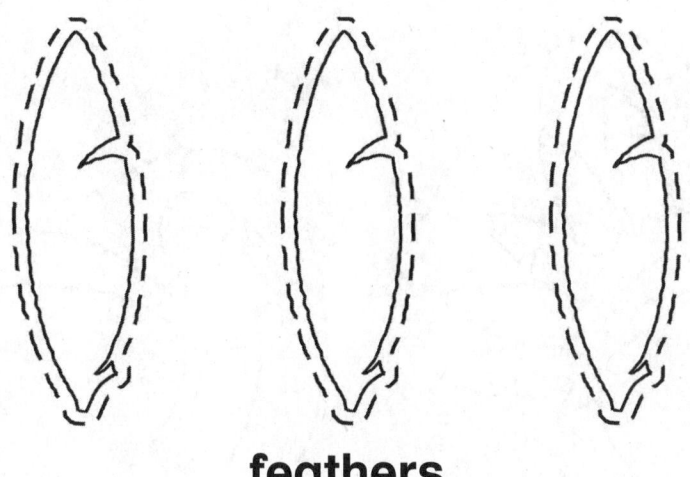

feathers

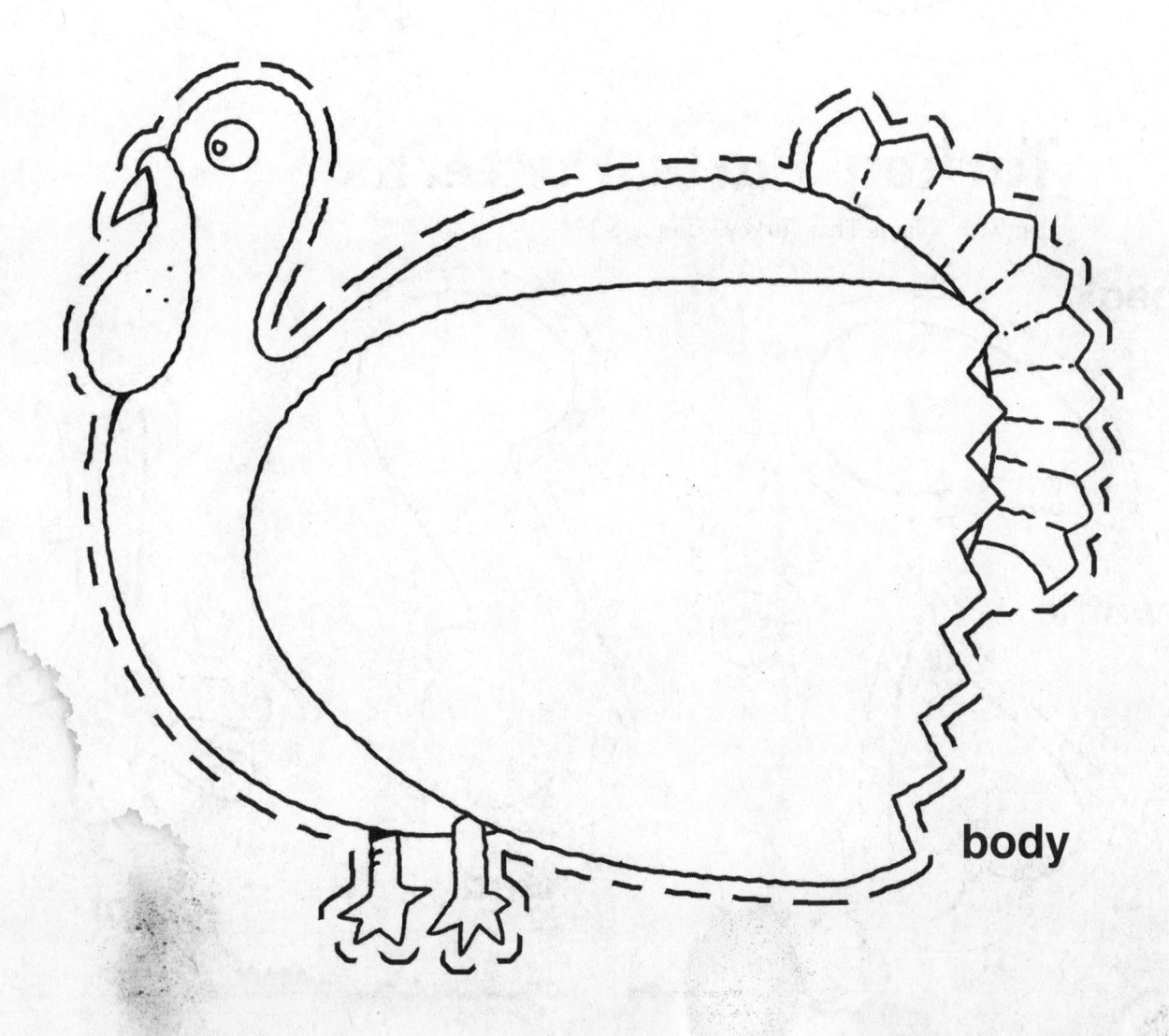

body

# Complete Turkey Patterns

Use with "Skip-Count Turkey" on page 16.

# Turkey Parts Patterns

Use with "Name That Turkey" on page 17

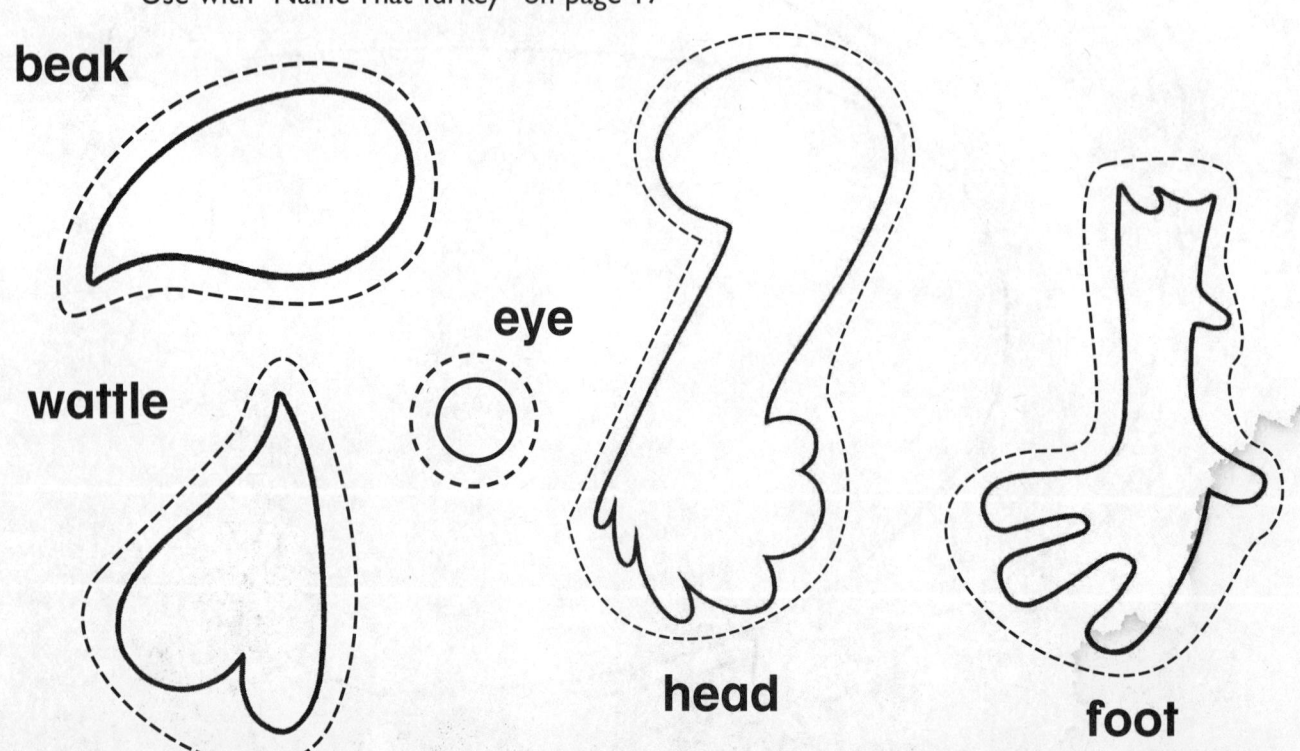

beak

wattle

eye

head

foot

www.harcourtschoolsupply.com
© Harcourt Achieve Inc. All rights reserved.

22

Unit 2, Thankful for Thanksgiving: Patterns
Three Cheers for November 1–2, SV 9838-8

# Turkey Parts Patterns
Use with "Name That Turkey" on page 17.

body

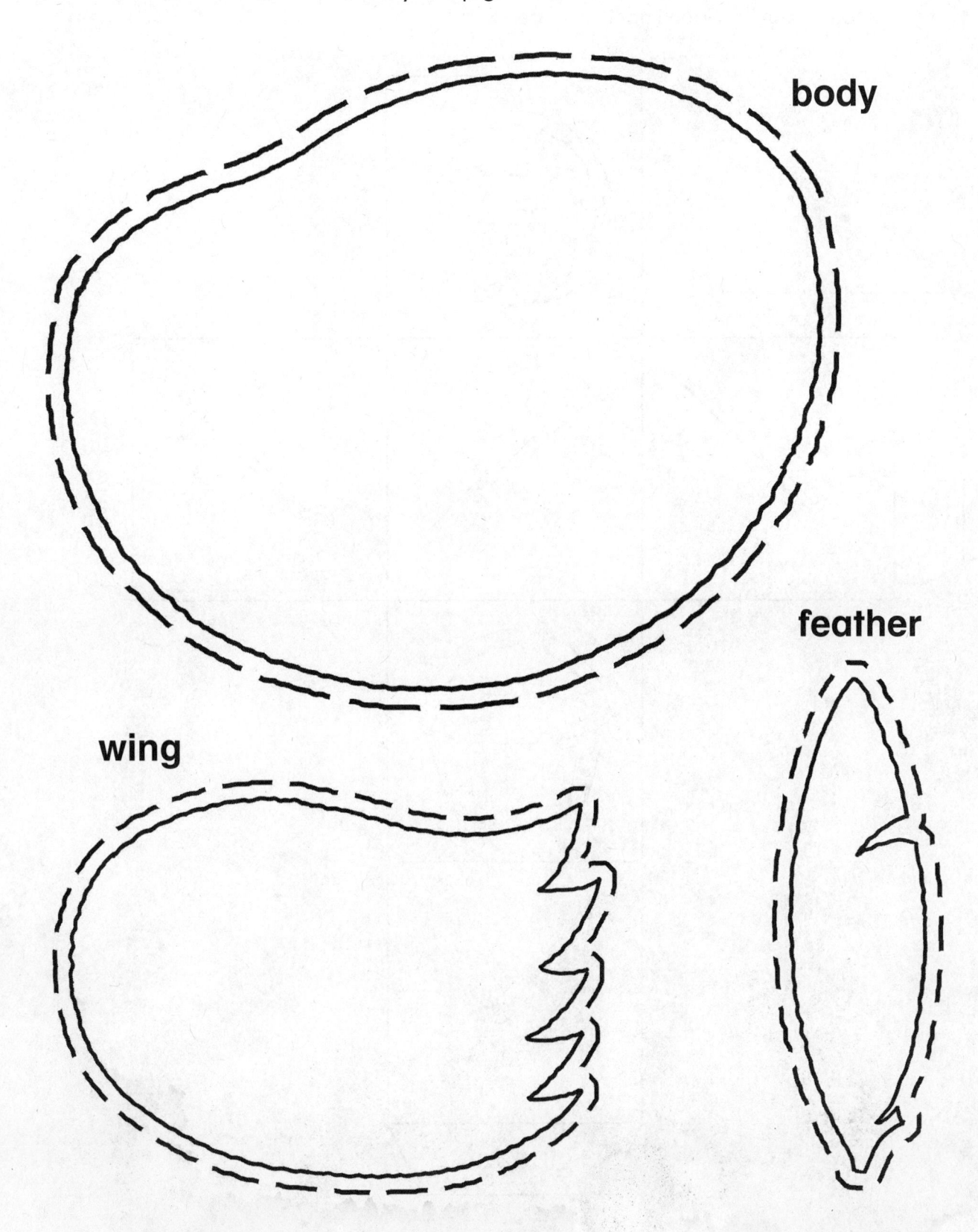

feather

wing

# Game Cube Pattern

Use with "Pilgrim Food Fun" on page 18 and "Building Blocks to Good Health . . . Good Food!" on page 75.

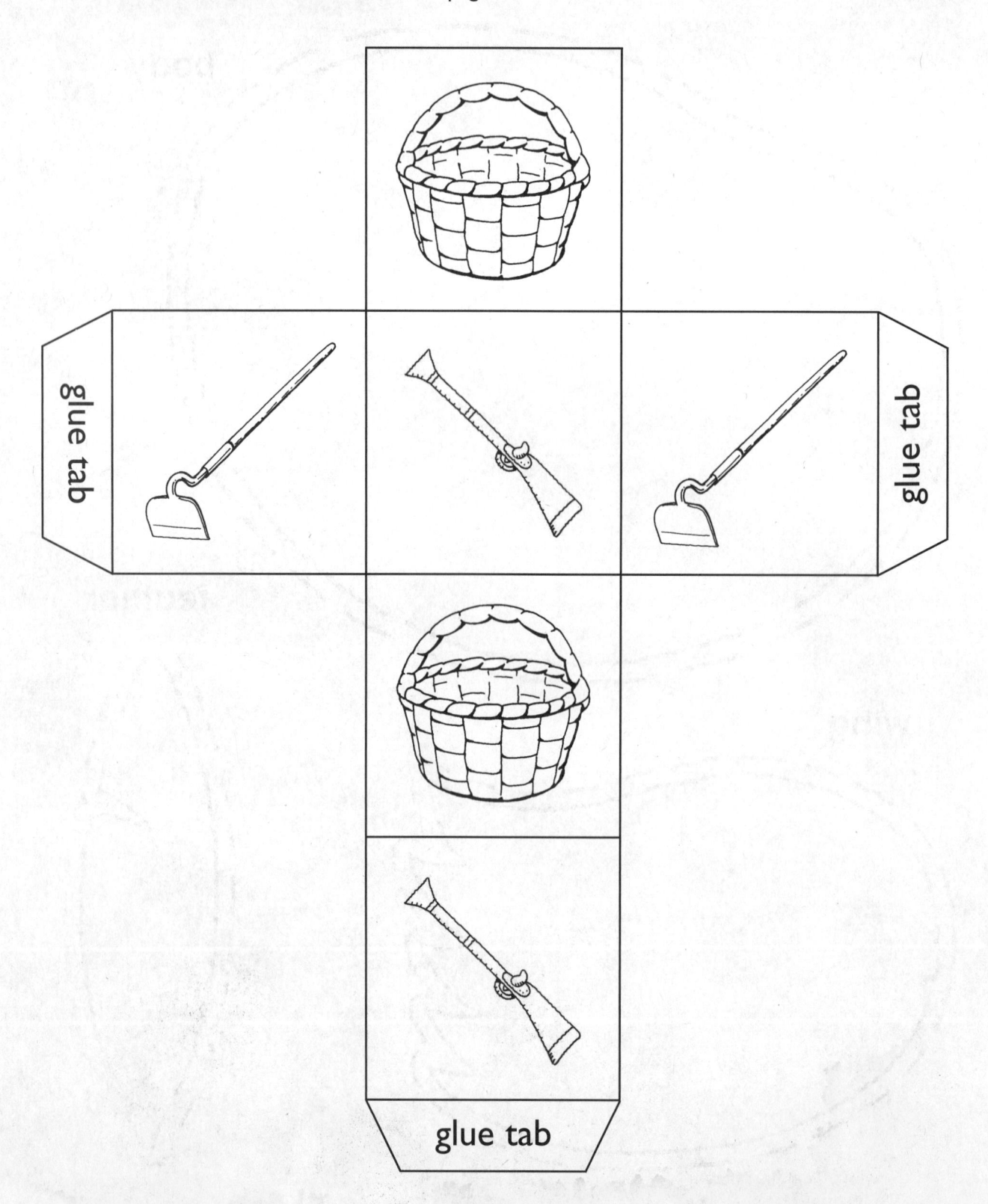

glue tab

glue tab

glue tab

# Food Picture Cards

Use with "Pilgrim Food Fun" on page 18.

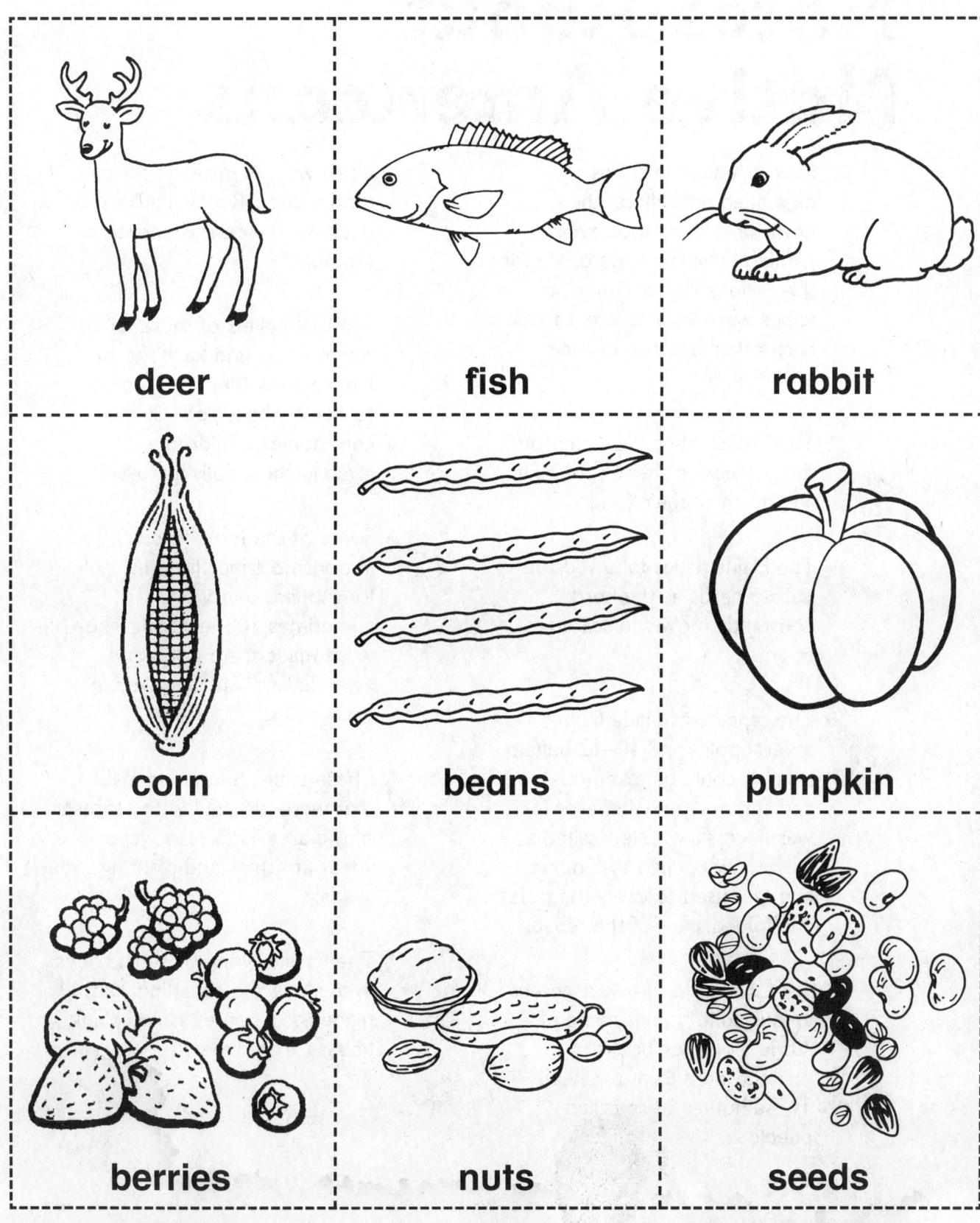

| | | |
|---|---|---|
| deer | fish | rabbit |
| corn | beans | pumpkin |
| berries | nuts | seeds |

# Notes About Native Americans

- Native American tribes depended entirely on their environment for food, shelter, and clothing. The ways of life for the various Native American tribes were very different from each other because of their environment.

- The Plains tribes depended on the buffalo for shelter, clothing, and much of their food.

- The Plains tribes followed the buffalo herds as the herds constantly moved in search of grass.

- The tepee was made from several poles and 10–12 buffalo skins. It could be taken down and set up again whenever it was necessary. A sled, called a travois, was pulled by a horse and was used to carry the poles and folded skins of the tepee.

- Tribes of the Southwest desert area lived in homes made of stone blocks or bricks to protect them from the heat. These homes were called pueblos.

- Corn was the most important food source. Rabbit, squirrel, or deer were eaten whenever available.

- Spiritual beliefs of these tribes revolved around kachinas, or nature gods. Men dressed up to depict these gods during ceremonies. Children were given kachina dolls as toys.

- Some of the Northeastern Woodland tribes lived in longhouses that were sometimes 100 feet long. They were made from poles and grass. Several families lived in each house.

- These tribes hunted animals that were plentiful in the forests of the area. They also were adept at fishing and planting seeds.

- The Pacific Northwestern tribes lived along the coastline. They made their homes, called plank houses, from trees.

# Paper Plate Dream Catcher

## Materials

- large paper plates
- yarn
- feathers
- craft beads
- scissors
- tape

## Directions

1. Cut out the center of a plate.
2. Use the scissors to make cuts that are ½ inch long around the edge of the plate.
3. Cut 2 long pieces of yarn.
4. Push the end of one piece of yarn into a cut. Tape the end to the back of the plate.
5. Cross the yarn to the cut that is opposite. Push the yarn into the cut.
6. Continue moving the yarn to the opposite cuts until the dream catcher is complete and looks like a bike-wheel spoke. Leave the remaining end hanging toward the bottom of the plate.
7. Weave the second piece of yarn in a spiral through the spokes of the dream catcher. Leave the remaining end hanging toward the bottom of the plate.
8. Tie the two ends of the two pieces of yarn around the bottom rim of the plate so that each end hangs down about one foot.
9. Put beads on each piece of yarn, pushing them up near the plate.
10. Tie a feather on each end. Then slide the beads over the knots.

# Buffalo Hide Tepee

## Materials

- poster on page 35
- large grocery bags
- crayons
- scissors
- clear tape
- rope
- five 7-foot poles, lumber, or PVC pipe
- markers

## Directions

**Teacher Preparation:** Duplicate and post the Native American symbols. Tie the tops of the poles together with rope to form the tepee frame. Discuss with children that Plains tribes used buffalo hides to make their tepees. Explain that they would draw symbols and pictures on the outside of the tepees to tell stories. Once children have completed their buffalo hides, allow them time to share the stories they wrote. Then help them tape the hides on the poles to finish the tepee. Leave an opening so that children can go inside.

1. Cut open a bag so it lies flat.
2. Cut the bag into a buffalo "hide" shape.
3. Draw symbols on the hide. Try to use the symbols to tell a story.

# Journey Cake

## You will need

- eggs
- milk
- cornmeal
- sugar
- salt
- vegetable oil spray
- bowls
- spoon
- pancake turner
- electric skillet
- measuring cups and spoons
- plates

## Directions

1. Beat 1 egg in a bowl.
2. Add 1 cup of milk and mix.
3. Mix together 1 cup of cornmeal, 1 teaspoon of sugar, and 1 teaspoon of salt in a separate bowl.
4. Add the cornmeal mixture to the milk mixture. Stir together.
5. Spray oil on the bottom of the skillet.
6. Ask an adult to heat the skillet to 350°F.
7. Ask the adult to pour some batter into the skillet to look like a pancake.
8. Have the adult turn the journey cake over when it is golden brown.
9. Remove the journey cake and put it on a plate.
10. Eat the journey cake when it is cool.

**Note:** Be aware of children who may have food allergies.

# Hopi Prayer
by Anonymous

Come here, Thunder, and look!

Come here, Cold, and see it rain!

Thunder strikes and makes it hot.

All seeds grow when it is hot.

Corn in blossom,

Beans in blossom,

Your face on garden looks,

Watermelon plant, muskmelon plant,

Your face on garden looks.

Aha-aha-ehe-ihe!

## Nifty Native Books

**Annie and the Old One**
by Miska Miles (Little, Brown & Company)

**Arrow to the Sun: A Pueblo Indian Tale**
by Gerald McDermott (Puffin)

**A Boy Called Slow: The True Story of Sitting Bull**
by Joseph Bruchac (Putnam)

**Brother Eagle, Sister Sky**
by Susan Jeffers (Puffin)

**Corn Is Maize: The Gift of the Indians**
by Aliki (HarperCollins)

**The Gift of the Sacred Dog**
by Paul Goble (Simon & Schuster)

**The Girl Who Loved Wild Horses**
by Paul Goble (Simon & Schuster)

**Houses of Bark: Tipi, Wigwam, and Longhouse**
by Bonnie Shemie (Tundra Books)

**Knots on a Counting Rope**
by Bill Martin (Henry Holt & Company)

**Sioux: Nomadic Buffalo Hunters**
by Rachael A. Koestler-Grack (Blue Earth Books)

**Sky Dogs**
by Jane Yolen (Harcourt Brace)

# Totally Terrific Totem Poles

## Materials

- pattern on page 36
- picture resources for totem poles (books or Internet)
- border
- green and white craft paper
- brown construction paper
- construction paper scraps
- markers
- stapler
- scissors
- glue

## Directions

**Teacher Preparation:** Cover the bulletin board with the green craft paper. Use a green marker to draw large evergreens on the top half of the paper. Add a border. Enlarge and trace three houses on the white craft paper. Cut them out and staple to the board. Add the caption along the bottom of the board.

1. Look at pictures of totem poles. Find a face that you like.
2. Get a sheet of brown paper. Place it on the table horizontally.
3. Draw and cut out parts from the paper scraps to make the totem pole face that you like.
4. Glue the parts in the center of the paper. Set the face aside to dry.
5. Overlap the edges and staple them together to form a cylinder.

Discuss with children the history of totem poles and how they are carved. Help groups of children stack and staple their completed faces to make totem poles. Help children glue or staple the totem poles in front of the houses.

# Native American Centers

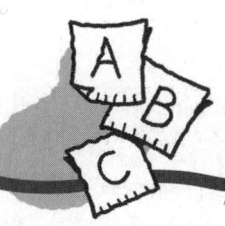

### Language Center

**Language Standard**
Uses alphabetical order

## Picture This Order

### Materials
- activity master on page 37
- sentence strips
- crayons
- glue
- scissors

**Teacher Preparation:** Duplicate the activity master for each child.

Review each picture name. Then have children color, cut out, and glue the pictures in ABC order on a sentence strip.

### Math Center

**Math Standard**
Develops fluency with basic number combinations for addition and subtraction

## Fact Family Fishing

### Materials
- patterns on page 38
- file folder
- scissors
- brown and gray construction paper
- marker
- laminate

**Teacher Preparation:** Duplicate and cut out six brown baskets and 24 gray fish. Choose the fact families you wish children to work with. Write the numbers used in those fact families on the baskets. Write the four related number facts on separate fish cutouts. Set the baskets on the folder in a pleasing arrangement and laminate them in place. Carefully slide a scissor blade along the top of each basket to make a pocket opening.

Have children match the four fish number facts to their basket.

# Native American Centers

### Science Center

**Science Standard**
Collects information using tools

## Corn Necklaces

### Materials

- hand lenses
- tweezers
- fishing line
- water
- paper towels
- ears of dried corn in a variety of colors
- large, dull craft needles
- scissors
- containers

**Teacher Preparation:** Several days in advance, pull the kernels off of several ears of corn and soak them in a container of water.

Have children examine the dried ears of corn and the wet kernels of corn. Invite them to use tweezers to pull apart a wet kernel of corn in order to examine the skin and the seed inside. Then have them cut a piece of fishing line and thread it on a needle. Have children string the wet kernels of corn to make a necklace.

### Social Studies Center

**Social Studies Standard**
Discusses how types of houses vary

## Native American Shelters

### Materials

- activity master on page 39
- crayons

**Teacher Preparation:** Duplicate the activity master for each child.

Discuss that the Native Americans used things in nature around them to live. Then name the kinds of homes on the activity master. Have children draw lines to match each shelter to its environment. Children can color the pictures if they wish.

# Native American Centers

**Writing Center**

**Language Arts Standard**
Understands that written words are separated by spaces

## All in the Clan

### Materials
- activity master on page 40
- crayons

**Teacher Preparation:** Duplicate the activity master for each child.

Explain that some families formed their own clans, or groups, in tribes that were very big. Often the clans associated themselves with an animal or plant because they thought they had its characteristics. For example, a bear clan believed its members were strong, powerful hunters, like the bear. Invite children to choose an animal they think they are most like. Have them draw and color a picture of the animal and write sentences telling why they think they are like that animal.

**Art Center**

**Art Standard**
Uses a variety of materials to produce drawings, paintings, prints, and constructions

## Pots and Paints

### Materials
- clay
- paintbrushes
- water
- pencils
- tempera paints
- containers for paints
- paper towels

**Teacher Preparation:** Set up the paint center.

Tell children that Native Americans in the Southwest were known for the clay pots they made. Show them how to make a pinch pot by rolling a ball of clay and inserting a thumb in the middle. Have them make the opening bigger by continuously turning the ball and lightly pinching the edges. Have children use a pencil to scratch their initials in the bottom of the pot. Then set the pots aside for several days to dry. Allow children to paint the pots when they are dry.

# Native American Centers

## Communication Center

**Language Arts Standard**
Connects ideas and experiences with those of others through speaking and listening

### Book Report

**Materials**

- fiction and nonfiction books related to Native Americans
- drawing paper
- crayons

**Teacher Preparation:** Gather a variety of books and place them in the center.

Invite children to read several books and then choose the one they like best. Have them draw a picture of their favorite part. Then ask children to take turns giving a brief book report.

## Game Center

**Social Studies Standard**
Follows rules, such as taking turns

### Which Hand?

**Materials**

- craft sticks
- markers

Tell children that a popular Native American game was called "Which Hand?" Partners would use two small sticks. One of the sticks had a hole in it. A person would put a stick in each hand, carefully covering the hole. The other person would guess which hand was holding the stick with the hole. If the guess was correct, partners switched roles.

Invite pairs of children to get two sticks. Have them draw a circle in the center on each side of one stick to represent the hole. Have them play Which Hand?

# Symbol Patterns Poster

Use with "Buffalo Hide Tepee" on page 27.

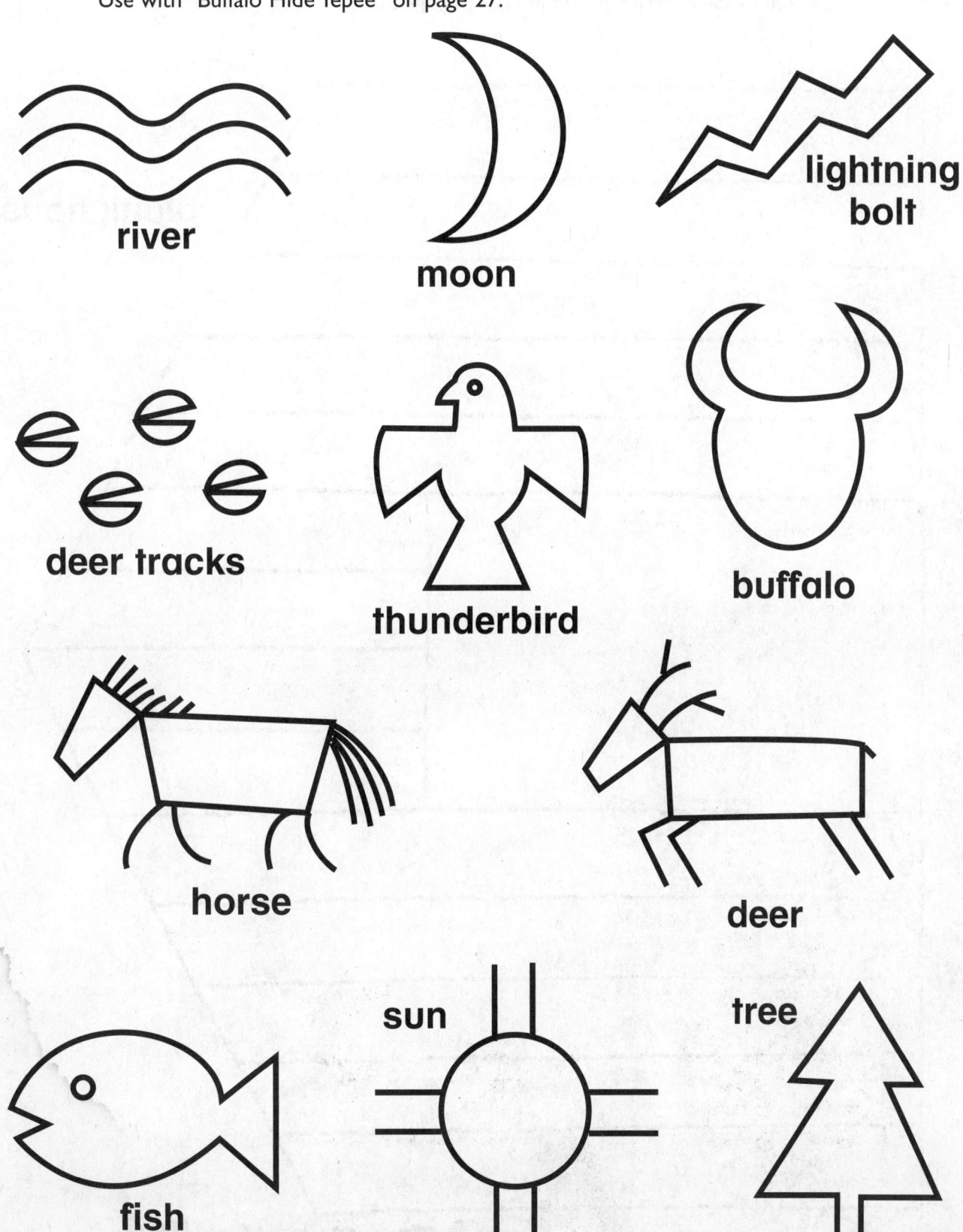

river

moon

lightning bolt

deer tracks

thunderbird

buffalo

horse

deer

fish

sun

tree

# Plank House Pattern

Use with "Totally Terrific Totem Poles" on page 30.

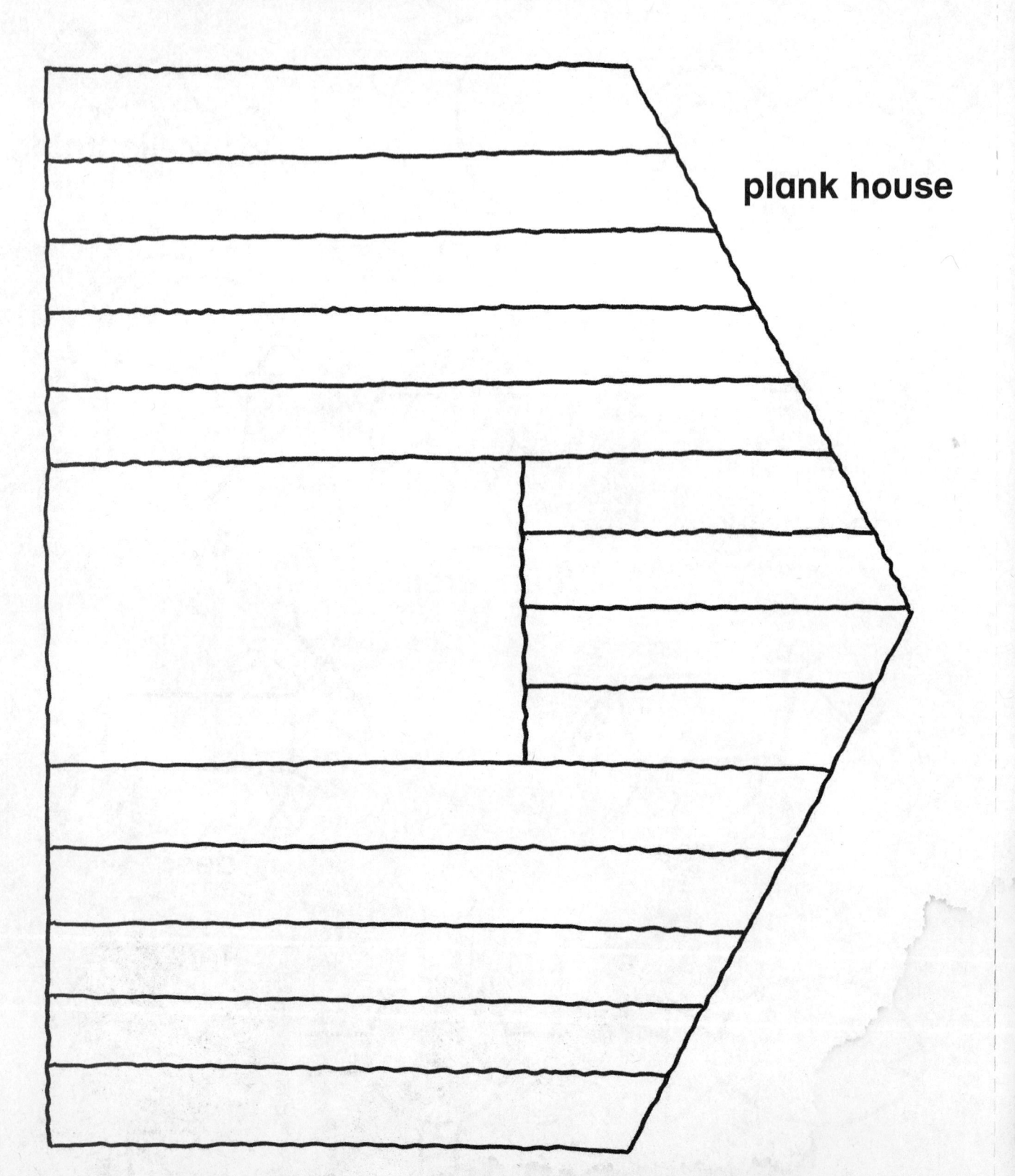

plank house

Name _____  Date _____

# ABC Order

**Directions:** Color and cut out the pictures. Glue them in ABC order.

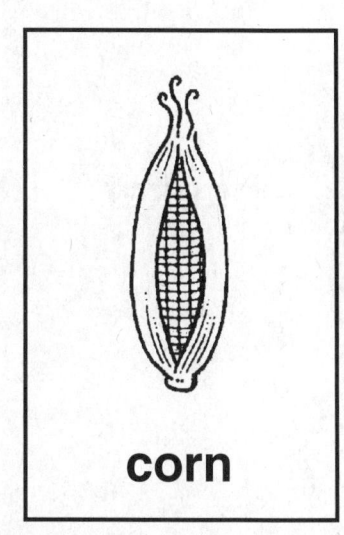

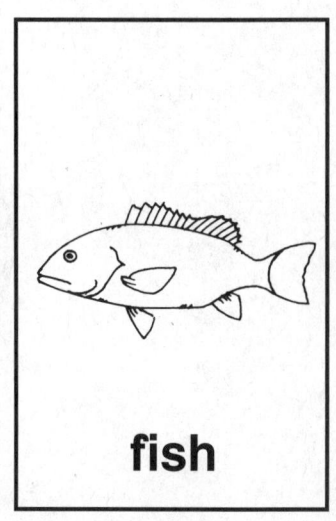

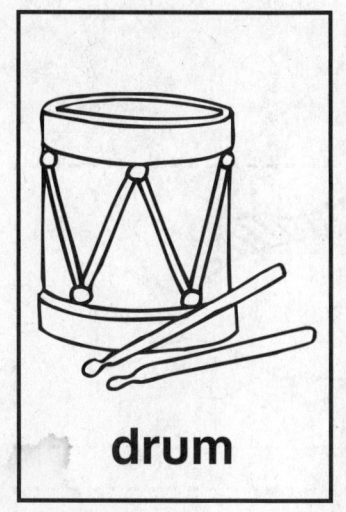

| corn | buffalo | tepee | fish |

| drum | horse | pot | tree |

Use with "Picture This Order" on page 31.

www.harcourtschoolsupply.com
© Harcourt Achieve Inc. All rights reserved.

Unit 3, Knowing Native Americans: Activity Master
Three Cheers for November 1–2, SV 9838-8

# Basket and Fish Patterns

Use with "Fact Family Fishing" on page 31.

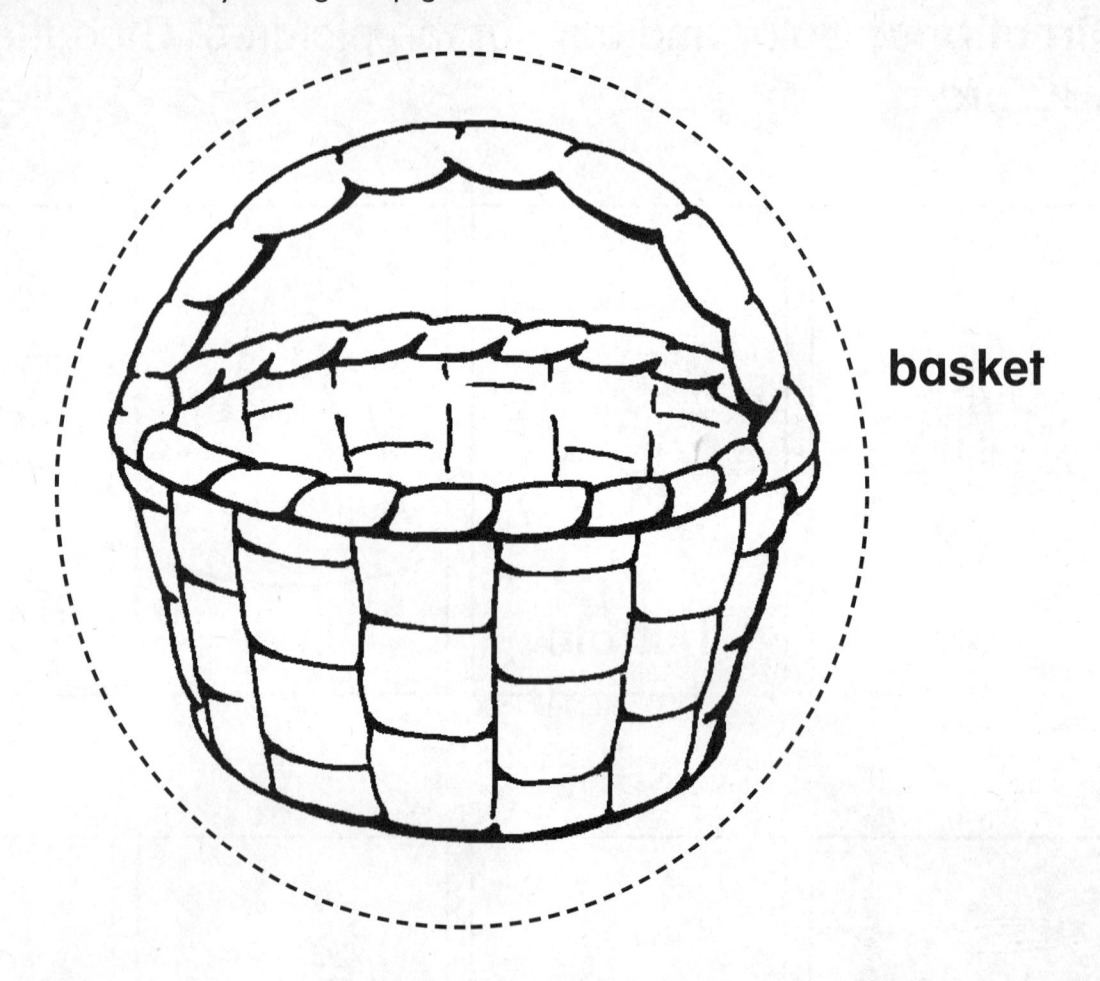

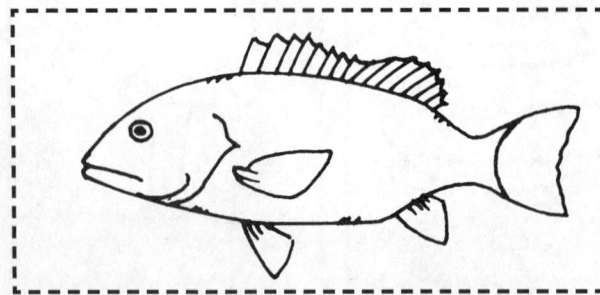

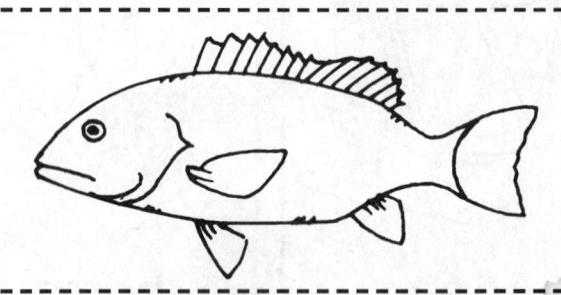

basket

fish

Name _____  Date _____

# Native American Homes

**Directions:** Draw lines to match each Native American shelter with the land where it could be found.

1.

2.

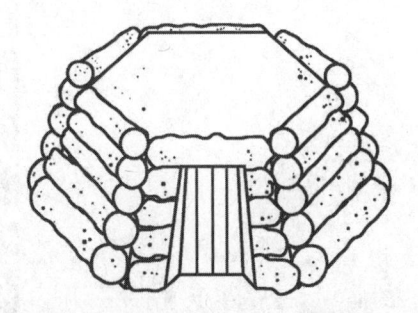

3.

4.

Use with "Native American Shelters" on page 32.

Name _____  Date _____

# A Clan for Me

**Directions:** What animal are you like? Draw a picture of it. Write sentences to tell why you are like the animal.

_____
_____
_____
_____

Use with "All in the Clan" on page 33.

# Meet the Mammals

- Mammals are animals that have three middle ear bones and hair. They are warmblooded and feed milk to their young.

- Some modern-day mammals include humans, apes, cats, bats, dogs, tigers, mice, aardvarks, beavers, elephants, gorillas, sloths, pandas, hamsters, horses, whales, and dolphins.

- Some mammals lay eggs. They belong to a group called monotremes. Spiny anteaters and duck-billed platypuses belong to this group.

- Marsupials are another group of mammals. Marsupial babies are underdeveloped when they are born and most often live in their mother's pouch for the first part of their lives. The koala, kangaroo, and numbat are marsupials.

- Mammals live all over the world. Their warmbloodedness helps them adapt to many kinds of environments and temperatures.

- Mammals have to eat a lot to maintain their high body temperature.

- Due to their specialized teeth, mammals are able to eat a huge variety of food sources.

- Herbivores are mammals that eat plants. Beavers, cows, horses, pandas, and sloths are herbivores.

- Carnivores are meat eaters. Whales, dolphins, dogs, and tigers are carnivores.

- Omnivores eat plants and meat. Some examples of omnivores are humans and some bears.

- Insectivores eat insects. Aardvarks, anteaters, and pangolins are insectivores.

- Anteaters are the only mammals that have no teeth.

- The fastest mammal is the cheetah. It can run with bursts of speed up to 60–70 miles per hour.

- The fastest mammal in water is the killer whale.

- The slowest mammal is the sloth. It travels less than 1 mile an hour.

# A Whale of a Sight!

## Materials

- small paper bags
- newspaper
- gray construction paper
- gray tempera paint
- paintbrushes
- containers for paint
- tape
- scissors
- glue
- markers

## Directions

**Teacher Preparation:** Set up a paint station with gray paint. You may wish to display the completed whales by hanging them from the ceiling.

1. Crumple several pieces of newspaper and place them in the bag until the bag is half full.
2. Tape the bag closed, leaving room to bend the end of the bag into a whale tail shape.
3. Paint the bag gray. Set it aside to dry.
4. Cut out flippers from gray construction paper for the whale. Fold the ends.
5. Glue the folded ends of the flippers to the sides of the bag.
6. Use markers to draw a face on the bottom of the bag.

# Mammal Homes

## Materials

- resources about mammals and the environments in which they live
- shoe boxes
- construction paper
- arts and crafts supplies
- paint
- paintbrushes
- containers for paint
- markers
- glue
- tape
- scissors

## Directions

**Teacher Preparation:** Set up a center with arts and crafts supplies. Set up a paint center. You may wish to pair children.

1. Choose a mammal. Read about the environment, or place, in which it lives.
2. Get a shoe box. Paint the inside to match the mammal's environment. For example, use green for a forest environment and white for an arctic environment.
3. Use the art supplies to make details to show the environment. Glue or tape the details in the box. For example, you might cut out trees from green paper or make brown paper balls to use as rocks.
4. Draw and cut out a picture of your mammal to add to the box.

# Mammal Sandwich

## You will need

- wheat bread
- creamy peanut butter or cream cheese
- black and brown icing tint
- coconut
- raisins
- craft sticks
- mammal-shaped cookie cutters
- paper plates
- containers

## Directions

**Teacher Preparation:** Use the brown and black tint to dye some of the coconut in separate containers.

1. Choose a cookie cutter for the shape of your sandwich.
2. Use a cookie cutter to cut out the animal shape from the bread.
3. Spread peanut butter or cream cheese on the bread.
4. Sprinkle coconut that is the same color as the animal's fur on the topping.
5. Use raisins to make a nose and an eye.

**Note:** Be aware of children who may have food allergies.

# Mammal Rap

We belong to the mammal family.
Let me tell you just what that means.

We all grow hair, and we drink milk, too.
Most have teeth that will help us chew.
Some mammals eat plants, and some eat meat.
Some mammals think that both are a tasty treat!

We belong to the mammal family.
Let me tell you just what that means.

Our blood is warm, I'm sure you've heard,
Which helps us live all over the world.
You can find us in the sea, on the land, in the sky.
We walk, we swim, we jump, we fly.

We belong to the mammal family.
Now you see how special we can be.

## Marvelous Mammal Books

**Creatures Small and Furry**
by Donald J. Crump
(National Geographic Society)

**Eye Wonder: Mammals**
by Sarah Walker (DK Publishing)

**Forest Mammals**
by Bobbie Kalman (Crabtree Publishing)

**Is a Camel a Mammal?**
by Tish Rabe (Random House)

**Mammal**
by Steve Parker (DK Publishing)

**Mammals**
by Joy Richardson (Watts Franklin)

**Mammals**
by Stephen Savage (Raintree Publishers)

**Marsupial Sue**
by John Lithgow (Simon & Schuster)

**Never Grab a Deer by the Ear**
by Colleen Stanley Bare (Dutton)

**Pinduli**
by Janell Cannon (Harcourt Brace)

**What Is a Marine Mammal?**
by Bobbie D. Kalman (Crabtree Publishing)

**Zipping, Zapping, Zooming Bats**
by Ann Earle (HarperCollins)

# Mammal Munchies

**Mammals That Eat Plants**

**Mammals That Eat Animals**

**Mammals That Eat Plants And Animals**

## Materials

- mammal picture cards on pages 50 and 51
- craft paper
- border
- sentence strips
- white construction paper
- crayons
- stapler
- scissors
- marker
- glue

## Directions

**Teacher Preparation:** Cover the bulletin board with craft paper. Divide the board into thirds with a marker. Add the border and caption. Write on sentence strips *Mammals That Eat Plants*, *Mammals That Eat Animals*, and *Mammals That Eat Plants and Animals*. Staple the strips at the bottom of each column. Duplicate multiple copies of the animal cards on construction paper and cut them apart.

1. Choose and color an animal card or draw a picture of a mammal. If you choose a card, glue the picture on a sheet of paper.
2. Draw pictures beside the mammal to show what it eats.

Have children staple their pictures in the correct column of the bulletin board.

# Mammal Centers

## Writing Center

**Language Standard**
Identifies and writes simple sentences

### It's a Fact

**Materials**

- resources about mammals
- drawing paper
- crayons

Invite children to choose a mammal they think is interesting and use resources to learn about it. Have children draw a picture of it. Then tell children to find two facts about the mammal and write them under the drawing.

## Art Center

**Art Standard**
Uses a variety of materials to produce drawings, paintings, prints, and constructions

### Milk and Mammals

**Materials**

- milk
- small paintbrushes
- white construction paper
- food color
- plastic cups

**Teacher Preparation:** Fill the cups half full with milk. Add food color to the milk to make the desired colors.

Remind children that mammals feed their babies milk. Then invite children to paint pictures of baby mammals on the construction paper.

# Mammal Centers

**Literacy Center**

**Language Arts Standard**
Uses synonyms, antonyms, and homonyms

## A Look at Antonyms

### Materials
- activity master on page 55

**Teacher Preparation:** Duplicate the activity master for each child.

Explain to children that antonyms are words that have opposite meanings. Then give examples related to mammals. For example, tell children that the cheetah is a fast animal and the sloth is a slow animal. Then have children complete the crossword puzzle.

**Technology Center**

**Technology Standard**
Applies keyword searches to acquire information

## Big and Small

### Materials
- computer
- chart paper
- marker

**Teacher Preparation:** Write the mammal names *African elephant, pigmy shrew, cheetah,* and *sloth* on chart paper. Set the chart in the technology center.

Tell children that the African elephant is the largest land animal and the pigmy shrew is the smallest. Also, tell children that the cheetah is the fastest animal, and the sloth is the slowest. Have children do an Internet search to find pictures of the animals to see what they look like.

# Mammal Picture Cards

Use with "Mammal Munchies" on page 45 and "Sounds Like Mammal Names" on page 46.

| | |
|---|---|
| bat | bear |
| dog | dolphin |
| ferret | fox |
| kangaroo | koala |

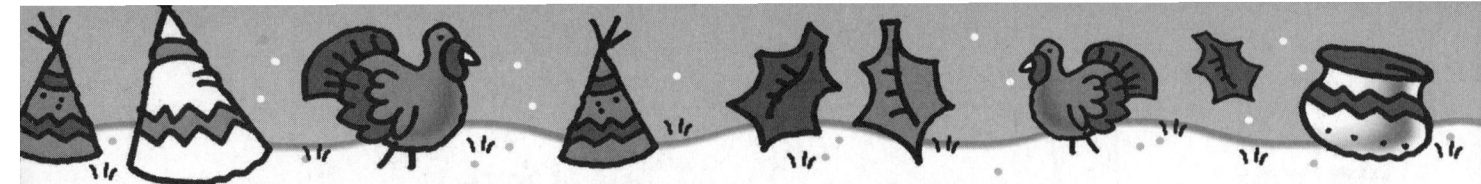

# Mammal Picture Cards

Use with "Mammal Munchies" on page 45 and "Sounds Like Mammal Names" on page 46.

| | |
|---|---|
| boy | monkey |
| rabbit | reindeer |
| skunk | squirrel |
| walrus | wolf |

Name _____  Date _____

# Zoo Time Treasure

**Directions:** Use an inch ruler. Write how many inches apart the pictures are. Color the pictures.

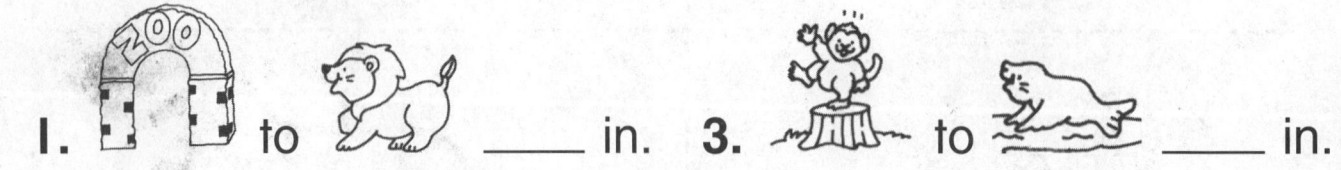

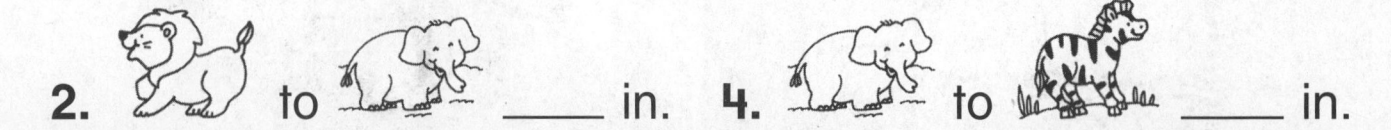

1. 🏛️ to 🦁 ____ in.
2. 🦁 to 🐘 ____ in.
3. 🐵 to 🦭 ____ in.
4. 🐘 to 🦓 ____ in.

Use with "Mammals at the Zoo" on page 46.

Name _____   Date _____

# Hairy Facts

**Directions:** Read the paragraph. Then color the pictures of the animals that are mammals.

A mammal is a kind of animal. It has hair on its body. The hair can be thick or thin. A rabbit's hair is thick. It is called fur. Fur helps keep the rabbit warm. A sheep has thick hair called wool. The elephant and the monkey have thin hair.

Use with "Pick the Mammals" on page 47.

Name _____  Date _____

# Feeding on the Farm

**Directions:** A farmer feeds her animals. Follow the arrows. Write the word that tells the direction she goes.

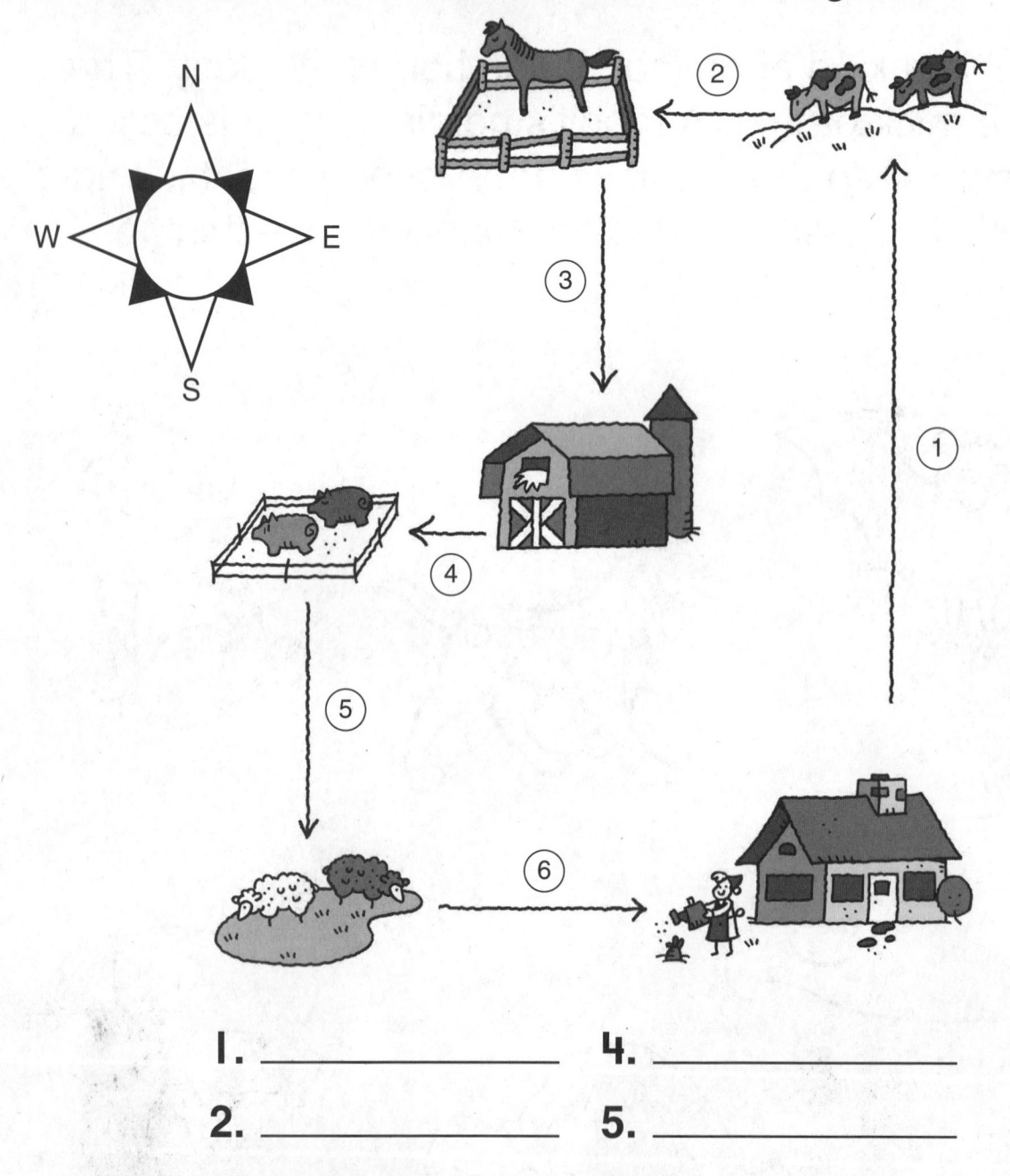

1. _____   4. _____
2. _____   5. _____
3. _____   6. _____

Use with "Directions on the Farm" on page 47.

Name _____  Date _____

# Mammal Opposites

**Directions:** Read each clue. Write a word from the box that means the opposite. Then write the word in the puzzle.

| fast | little | quiet | run | tall | thin |

**Across**
1. slow
4. big
6. walk

**Down**
2. short
3. loud
5. thick

Use with "A Look at Antonyms" on page 49.

# Election and Voting Facts

An election is an event in which people vote among candidates to fill a government office or position.

The basic process of voting in an election is described in the U.S. Constitution.

The United States has a democratic government. People vote for candidates who will make the rules and work to keep the country and the citizens safe.

A polling place is where people go to vote.

To vote, a person must be 18 years or older and a U.S. citizen.

A candidate is a person who seeks or is nominated for an office or position.

Candidates campaign to get elected. They make speeches, participate in debates, and talk to people. They make posters, buttons, and advertisements for the television and the radio.

People record their votes on a ballot. The ballot lists all the candidates and the office they are running for.

There are several kinds of ballots. Some voters use a pencil to mark boxes by the candidate's name. Others use a voting machine to make a hole by the candidate's name. The ballot is secret and is placed in the ballot box.

Some voting machines look and work like a computer. No paper or pencils are used. The vote is counted electronically.

There are many elections at the local level. Voters help decide new laws, transportation issues, judgeships, school board officials, and city and state officials.

A President is elected to oversee national policies. A governor is elected to oversee a state's policies. A mayor is elected to oversee a city's policies.

# Ballot Box

## Materials

shoe boxes; craft paper in a variety of colors; scrap construction paper in a variety of colors; art supplies, such as foiled star and flag stickers, yarn, and glitter; markers; scissors; matte knife; tape; glue

## Directions

**Teacher Preparation:** Use the matte knife to cut a slit in the top of each shoe box. Cut the craft paper to a size that will wrap the shoe boxes. Have children work in groups of three or four. Each box will serve as a polling place at the end of the week.

1. With your group members, discuss patriotic colors and symbols of the United States.
2. Wrap the top and bottom of the box separately using the craft paper. Cut out the slit in the box top.
3. Use the art supplies to decorate the ballot box. Be creative!

---

# Candidate Button

## Materials

activity master on page 65, patterns on page 66, construction paper in a variety of colors, foiled star stickers, curling ribbon, contact paper, pin backs, markers and crayons, scissors, glue, round container lids, hot glue gun, glue sticks

## Directions

**Teacher Preparation:** Duplicate the activity master for each child. Duplicate multiple copies of the button patterns on white construction paper.

1. Read the information about Super Dog and Great Cat. Decide whom you will vote for.
2. Color and cut out a picture of your candidate.
3. Choose a background color for your button.
4. Trace around a lid to make a circle. Cut it out.
5. Glue the picture of your candidate on the circle.
6. Decorate the button with markers and stickers.
7. Cover the button with contact paper. Trim off the extra contact paper.
8. Ask your teacher to glue the pin on the back of the button with hot glue.
9. Add ribbon curls to your pin if you wish.
10. Wear your button all week.

# Graham Cracker Ballots

## You will need
- graham crackers
- peanut butter or cream cheese
- rope licorice
- raisins
- craft sticks
- paper plates

## Directions
1. Spread the peanut butter or cream cheese on the whole graham cracker.
2. Use licorice to write *DOG* and *CAT*.
3. Which candidate do you like best—Super Dog or Great Cat? Put a raisin by that name.

**Note:** Be aware of children who may have food allergies.

# Candidate Chant

(Chorus)
Will the dog win or the cat?
The class will vote to decide all that!

Those who want to vote for Super Dog chant:
Super Dog is who we want.
He wants swings and extra play.
And as a very special treat,
Ice cream will be free Friday.

(Chorus)

Those who want to vote for Great Cat chant:
Great Cat is our candidate.
She's the one we want to run.
We'll get chocolate milk to drink,
And more computers will be fun.

(Chorus)

## Vote for These Books!

**America Votes: How Our President Is Elected**
by Linda Granfield (Kids Can Press, Limited)

**Ballot Box Battle**
by Emily Arnold McCully (Bantom Doubleday Dell)

**The Day Gogo Went to Vote**
by Eleanor Batezat Sisulu (Megan Tingley Books)

**Duck for President**
by Doreen Cronin (Simon & Schuster)

**Pete for President!**
by Daisy Alberto (The Kane Press)

**Presidential Elections and Other Cool Facts**
by Syl Sobel (Barron's Educational Series)

**Running for Public Office**
by Sarah E. De Cupua (Scholastic)

**So You Want to Be President?**
by Judith St. George (Philomel)

**Stuart Little: Think Big, Vote Little!**
by Laura Driscoll (HarperCollins)

**Vote!**
by Eileen Christelow (Houghton Mifflin)

**Voting and Elections**
by Patricia J. Murphy (Compass Point Books)

**What Presidents Are Made Of**
by Hanoch Piven (Simon & Schuster)

# Our Elected Leaders

## Materials

- recent newspapers and magazines
- craft paper
- red, white, and blue construction paper
- stapler
- border
- scissors
- crayons or markers

## Directions

**Teacher Preparation:** Cover the bulletin board with the craft paper. Add a border and the caption.

Review the offices and responsibilities of the President, governor, and mayor. Allow class time for children to find pictures of these people.

1. Cut out pictures of the President, governor, and mayor from newspapers and magazines. Glue them to a sheet of construction paper. Or draw and color pictures of these people on paper.

2. Write a caption for the picture, telling the name of the person and the office the person holds.

3. Share your pictures with the class.

4. Staple the pictures to the bulletin board.

Encourage children to look for other pictures of elected officials at home to add to the bulletin board.

www.harcourtschoolsupply.com
© Harcourt Achieve Inc. All rights reserved.

Unit 5, Take a Vote: Bulletin Board
Three Cheers for November 1–2, SV 9838-8

# Election Centers

## Language Center

**Language Arts Standard**
Decodes words by using letter-sound patterns

### The Sounds of g and s

**Materials**
- activity master on page 67

**Teacher Preparation:** Duplicate the activity master for each child.

Tell children that Super Dog and Great Cat are candidates for school president. Write these names on the chalkboard and encourage children to make the sound of each letter in the candidates' names.

Remind children that *super* begins with a hard s sound and *great* begins with a hard g sound. Review the sounds and spelling patterns for variant g and s. Then help children identify the pictures. Have children say the name of the picture at the beginning of each row. Tell them to listen for the sound of g or s. Then have them color two other pictures in that row whose names have the same g or s sound.

## Math Center

**Math Standard**
Develops and uses strategies for whole-number operations, with a focus on addition and subtraction

### Vote for Math

**Materials**
- patterns on page 68
- white construction paper
- scissors
- file folders
- markers
- glue

**Teacher Preparation:** Duplicate the ballot box and ballot patterns several times on construction paper. Cut them out and write facts or algorithms on the ballots and the answers on the boxes. Color the ballots and boxes if you wish. Glue the boxes in a pleasing arrangement on the inside of the file folders.

Have children match the ballots to the ballot boxes.

# Election Centers

## Science Center

**Science Standard**
Describes how technology is used

### Technology Helps

**Materials**
- activity master on page 69

**Teacher Preparation:** Duplicate the activity master for each child.

Discuss with children how candidates share information about themselves and about the things candidates do in a campaign. Then have children look at the different kinds of technology in the pictures and write a sentence telling how a candidate uses each during a campaign.

## Social Studies Center

**Social Studies Standard**
Locates places of significance on maps

### The President's Home

**Materials**
- United States wall map
- pictures of the White House, inside and out

Talk to children about the job of the President of the United States. Tell them that the President lives in Washington, D.C. Explain that the President and the President's family live in the White House. Show pictures of the White House.

Have children locate Washington, D.C. on the wall map.

# Election Centers

## Writing Center

**Language Standard**
Identifies and writes simple sentences

### Making a Change

**Materials**

- activity master completed in "Who Will You Vote For?" on page 65
- writing paper

Have children review what the candidates Super Dog and Great Cat would change in the school if they were elected school president. Then invite children to think of one or two things they would like to change if they were running for the office. Have them write sentences telling their ideas.

## Art Center

**Art Standard**
Places forms in orderly arrangement to create a design

### Make a Poster

**Materials**

- patterns on page 66
- 12 x 18 construction paper
- scissors
- crayons and markers

**Teacher Preparation:** Enlarge, duplicate, and cut apart the pictures.

Tell children that candidates display posters to tell people their names and the office they are running for. Sometimes a candidate includes a saying, or slogan, to catch the interest of the voter.

Invite children to make a poster for their candidate—Super Dog or Great Cat. They can use the patterns or draw the character on their own. Challenge children to write a catchy slogan about the candidate. Display the posters around the room.

# Election Centers

### Technology Center

**Social Studies Standard**
Uses voting as a way of making choices and decisions

## Time to Vote

### Materials
- ballot boxes completed in "Ballot Box" on page 57
- patterns on page 70
- hole punch

**Teacher Preparation:** Duplicate the ballot patterns and cut them apart. Place the ballot boxes and hole punch in the center.

Invite children to vote for their favorite candidate for school president—Super Dog or Great Cat. Have them place their ballots in the ballot boxes. Remind children that voting is supposed to be secret.

**Extension:** After everyone has voted, work together to count the ballots using tallies. Compile the data into a bar graph or picture graph using the character patterns on page 66.

### Communication Center

**Social Studies Standard**
Identifies characteristics of good citizenship

## A Good Leader

### Materials
- pictures of children in different group activities, including a sports game, on the playground, or in a store

**Teacher Preparation:** Place the pictures in the center.

Challenge children to discuss the characteristics that a good leader should have. They can look at the pictures to get ideas.

Name _____ Date _____

# Who Will You Vote For?

**Directions:** Super Dog and Great Cat both want to be school president. Read what each candidate wants to do. Who will you vote for? Color the picture.

**Super Dog**

- longer playground time each day
- free ice cream each Friday
- help the teacher one hour each week
- no homework on the weekends
- more swings on the playground
- people who break rules should clean the desks that day

**Great Cat**

- time on the computer each day
- free chocolate milk each Friday
- help clean the school each week
- no more than one subject of homework each day
- more computers in the classroom
- people who break rules should not get computer time that day

Use with "Candidate Button" on page 57 and with "Making a Change" on page 63.

# Super Dog and Great Cat Patterns

Use with "Candidate Button" on page 57 and "Make a Poster" on page 63.

**Super Dog**

**Great Cat**

Name _____    Date _____

# The Sounds of g and s

**Directions:** Say the name of the picture at the beginning of each row. Listen for the sound of *g* or *s*. Color two other pictures in that row whose names have the same sound. (Hint: The sound may not be at the beginning of the word.)

| | | | |
|---|---|---|---|
|  1. goat | 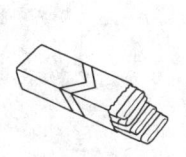 gum | 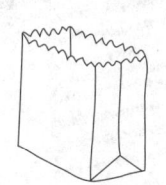 bag |  gerbil |
|  2. giraffe | 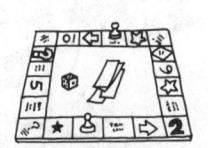 game |  giant |  cage |
|  3. sun | 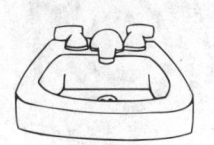 sink |  hose | 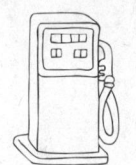 gas |
|  4. rose |  sock |  cheese | 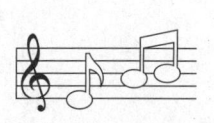 music |
|  5. sugar |  tissue |  seal |  mission |

Use with "The Sounds of g and s" on page 61.

# Ballots and Boxes Patterns

Use with "Vote for Math" on page 61.

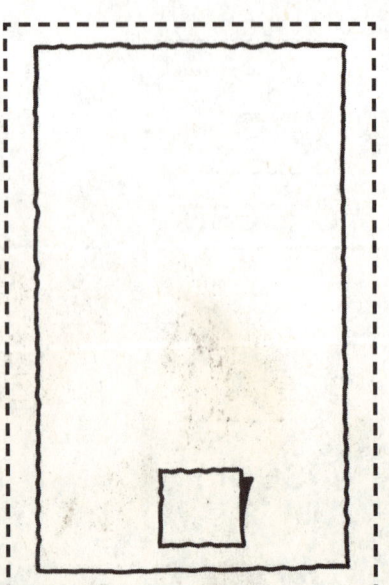

**ballot boxes**

**ballots**

Name _____  Date _____

# Sharing the News

**Directions:** Look at each picture. How can a candidate use it? Write a sentence.

1.  _____
   _____

2.  _____
   _____

3.  _____
   _____

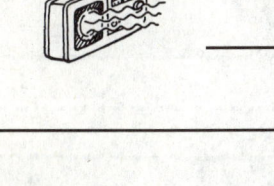

4.  _____
   _____

5.  _____
   _____

Use with "Technology Helps" on page 62.

www.harcourtschoolsupply.com
© Harcourt Achieve Inc. All rights reserved.

Unit 5, Take a Vote: Activity Master
Three Cheers for November 1–2, SV 9838-8

# Ballot Patterns

Use with "Time to Vote" on page 64.

# Good Food Facts

- The U.S. Department of Agriculture (USDA) created the Food Pyramid in 1991 as a guide for healthy eating.

- The Food Pyramid is currently under revision in order to better reflect recent research. Check the USDA website for updated information.

- The Food Pyramid suggests eating the recommended amounts from all of the food groups on a daily basis.

- Bread, cereals, rice, and pasta form a group of foods that provide vitamins, energy, and fiber needed for strong and healthy bodies.

- A variety of fruits and vegetables provide the necessary vitamins and minerals needed for healthy bodies.

- The main nutrient the body gets from the milk, yogurt, and cheese group is calcium. Calcium is essential for developing strong bones and teeth.

- Healthy bodies need protein and iron which can be provided by lean meats, poultry, fish, dry beans, eggs, and nuts.

- Fats are necessary for the body to create cell membranes and hormones and for the growth and functioning of vital organs.

- Fats and oils made from plant sources are healthier than those made from animal sources.

- Spinach contains folic acid. Without appropriate levels of folic acid, a person may feel sad.

- Chicken soup helps relieve the congestion that comes with a cold. Chicken has an amino acid that thins the mucous lining of the sinuses, relieving stuffiness.

- Garlic and onions kill cold and flu bacteria.

## You Are What You Eat Diary

### Materials
- white craft paper
- crayons
- tape
- scissors

### Directions

**Teacher Preparation:** Cut a piece of craft paper the length of each child. When the outlines are completed, tape them to the wall. Encourage children to track the foods they eat for several days.

1. Work with a partner. Take turns lying on a piece of craft paper. Trace the body.
2. Draw the parts of the face.
3. Draw pictures all over the body to show the foods eaten for each meal and snack.

**Extension:** After the children have finished recording their food consumption, suggest that they put an X on the foods that are not healthy.

## Pass Your Plate

### Materials
- paper plates
- recycled magazines
- scissors
- glue

### Directions

1. Cut out pictures of healthy foods that you like to eat. Be sure to include a meat, a vegetable, a fruit, bread or cereal, and milk or cheese.
2. Glue the pictures on a plate.
3. Tell a partner which group each food belongs to.

# A Healthy Tasty Taco Treat

## You will need
- taco shells
- browned hamburger meat
- diced tomatoes
- grated cheddar cheese
- diced lettuce
- salsa
- spoons
- paper plates
- napkins
- microwave or electric skillet

## Directions

**Teacher Preparation:** Heat the hamburger in a microwave or electric skillet.

Tell children that the most important foods that a body needs to stay healthy are in a taco. (Tell them that a tomato is really a fruit!)

1. Put a taco shell on a plate.
2. Spoon the cooked hamburger into the taco shell.
3. Sprinkle grated cheese on the meat.
4. Add lettuce and tomatoes on the meat.
5. Spoon salsa on top if you wish.

**Note:** Be aware of children who may have food allergies.

# Betty Botter

**Teacher Note:** Divide the class into two groups to read this tongue twister chorally.

**All:** Betty Botter bought some butter,
But she said,

**Group 1:** "The butter's bitter.
If I put it in my batter,
It will make my batter bitter.

**Group 2:** But a bit of better butter—
That would make my batter better."

**All:** So she bought a bit of butter,
Better than her bitter butter.

**Group 1:** And she put it in her batter,
**Group 2:** And the batter was not bitter.

**All:** So 'twas better Betty Botter
Bought a bit of better butter.

## Books to Bite Into

**Eat Healthy, Feel Great**
by William Sears (Little, Brown & Company)

**Eating the Alphabet: Fruits & Vegetables from A to Z**
by Lois Ehlert (Harcourt Brace)

**Food Fight!**
by Carol Diggory (Shields Handprint Books)

**Gregory the Terrible Eater**
by Mitchell Sharmat (Scholastic)

**Growing Vegetable Soup**
by Lois Ehlert (Harcourt Brace)

**Good Enough to Eat: A Kids' Guide to Food and Nutrition**
by Lizzy Rockwell (HarperCollins)

**Eat Your Vegetables! Drink Your Milk!**
by Alvin Silverstein (Scholastic)

**Little Red Hen**
by Paul Galdone (Houghton Mifflin Company)

**The Pizza That We Made**
by Joan Holub (Puffin)

**Stone Soup**
by Marcia Brown (Simon and Schuster)

**The Seven Silly Eaters**
by Mary Ann Hoberman (Harcourt)

**Tops and Bottoms**
by Janet Stevens (Harcourt)

# Building Blocks to Good Health...

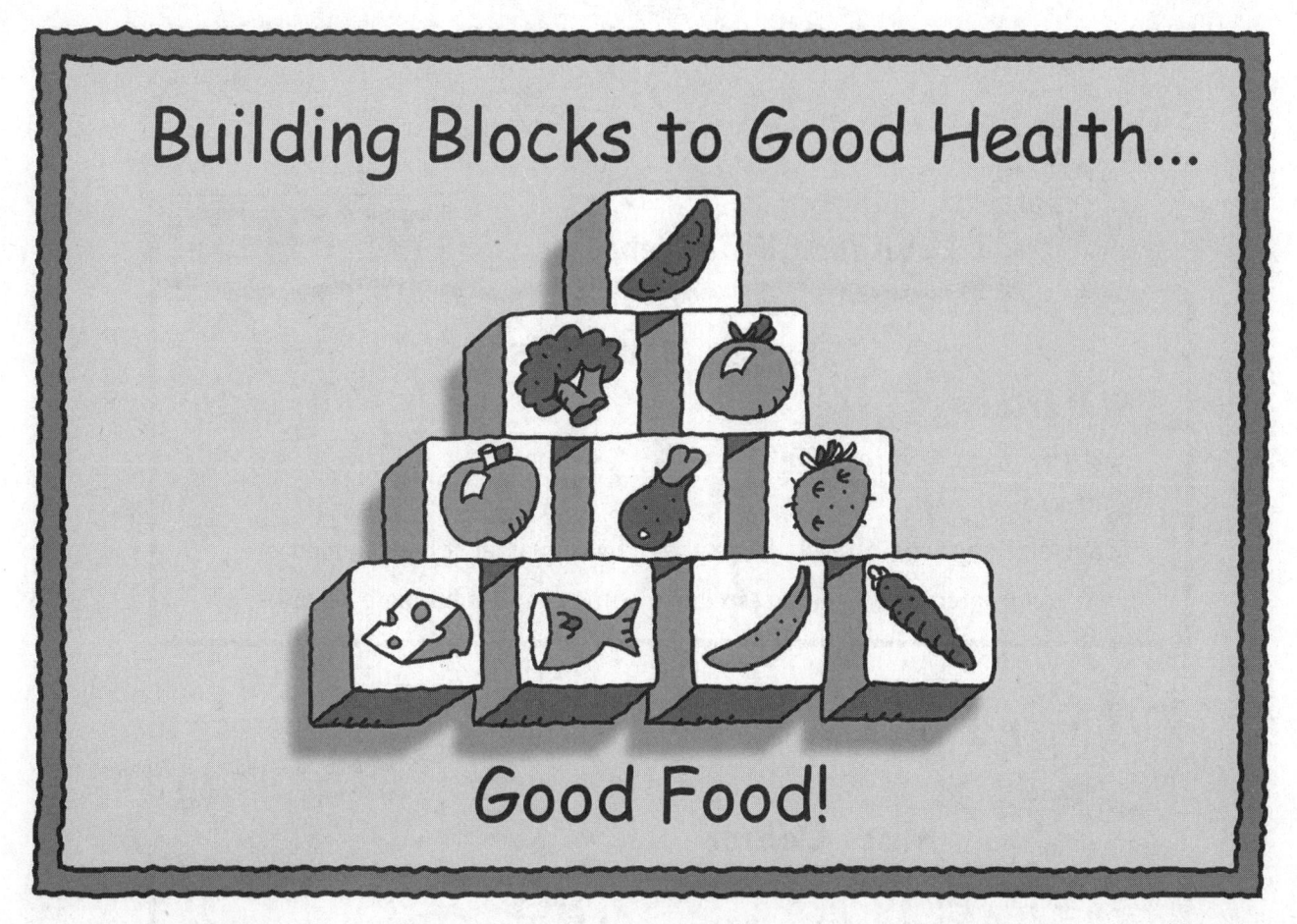

## Good Food!

## Materials

- pattern on page 24
- light colored construction paper
- craft paper
- border
- clear tape
- markers
- wide masking tape
- scissors

## Directions

**Teacher Preparation:** Cover the pictures on the cube pattern and duplicate the figure for each child. Cover the board with the craft paper. Add a decorative border and the caption.

1. Cut out the cube.
2. Draw pictures of healthy foods on five sides.
3. Fold the cube along the lines and tape the sides closed.

Invite children to identify the healthy foods they drew. Help them tape one side of the cube to the board to form a tower or pyramid.

# Food Centers

### Language Center

**Language Arts Standard**
Recognizes vowel sounds

## Long e Foods

### Materials
- activity master on page 80
- crayons

**Teacher Preparation:** Duplicate the activity master for each child.

Have children color the pictures whose names have the long e sound.

### Math Center

**Math Standard**
Represents data using concrete objects, pictures, and graphs

## Graphic About Vegetables

### Materials
- activity master on page 81
- crayons

**Teacher Preparation:** Duplicate the activity master for each child.

Have children complete the graph to show the number of each kind of vegetable.

# Food Centers

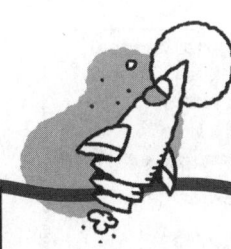

### Science Center

**Science Standard**
Sorts objects according to their characteristics

## Food Sort

### Materials

- picture cards on pages 82–83
- markers
- craft paper
- scissors

**Teacher Preparation:** Duplicate, color, and cut out the picture cards. Draw a large food pyramid on the craft paper and label the parts and serving amounts. Do not include pictures.

Have children identify the food on each card and match it to the appropriate food group on the food pyramid.

**Teacher note:** If the U.S. Department of Agriculture changes the Food Guide Pyramid, adjust the activity so that children match the food cards to the new standards.

### Social Studies Center

**Social Studies Standard**
Identify the role of markets in the exchange of goods and services

## Goods and Services

### Materials

- food containers
- coin and bill manipulatives
- calculator
- price tags
- toy cash register
- grocery bags

**Teacher Preparation:** Set up the center as a grocery store. Make price tags for the food containers.

Discuss the differences in goods and services. Ask children to identify the goods and services related to food. Then invite children to role-play buying goods in a store. Shoppers select an item and count out the correct coins and bills. Clerks provide change if needed.

# Food Centers

## Writing Center

**Language Arts Standard**
Writes in different forms for different purposes

### Recipe Writing

**Materials**
- activity master on page 84
- crayons

**Teacher Preparation:** Duplicate the activity master for each child.

Show children examples of recipes. Discuss the importance of listing the ingredients, their amounts, and listing the directions in sequence. Then invite children to draw a picture of their favorite food. Challenge them to write the recipe telling how to make it.

## Communication Center

**Health Standard**
Identifies and demonstrates the use of the five senses

### Using the Five Senses

**Materials**
- salty crackers
- hand lenses
- plastic knife
- American cheese
- paper plates

**Teacher Preparation:** Cut the cheese into squares.

Lead children in a discussion of the five senses and how they help us identify food. Then have children each take a cracker and a slice of cheese. Ask partners to examine the two foods and describe how their senses help them identify the foods. Then invite them to enjoy the cracker snack.

**Note:** Be aware of children who may have food allergies.

# Food Centers

### Game Center

> **Health Standard**
> Describes activities that enhance individual health such as nutrition

## A-Maze-ing Food

### Materials
- activity master on page 85

**Teacher Preparation:** Duplicate the activity master for each child.

Ask children to help the boy get to the restaurant by drawing a line to it.

### Physical Development Skills Center

> **Physical Education Standard**
> Describes food as a source of energy

## Energy to Move

### Materials
no materials needed

Explain to children that the body needs healthy foods to give it the energy to move. Compare it to the way a car needs gas. Then review healthy foods and unhealthy foods. Invite children to listen to food names that you call out. If the food is healthy, tell children to run in place as fast as they can. If the food is not healthy, they should stand still.

Name _____ Date _____

# Time to Eat

**Directions:** Color the pictures whose names have the long *e* sound.

Use with "Long e Foods" on page 76.

www.harcourtschoolsupply.com
© Harcourt Achieve Inc. All rights reserved.

80

Unit 6, Food and You: Activity Master
Three Cheers for November 1–2, SV 9838-8

Name _____ Date _____

# Food Graph

**Directions:** Color a box in the graph for each vegetable below.

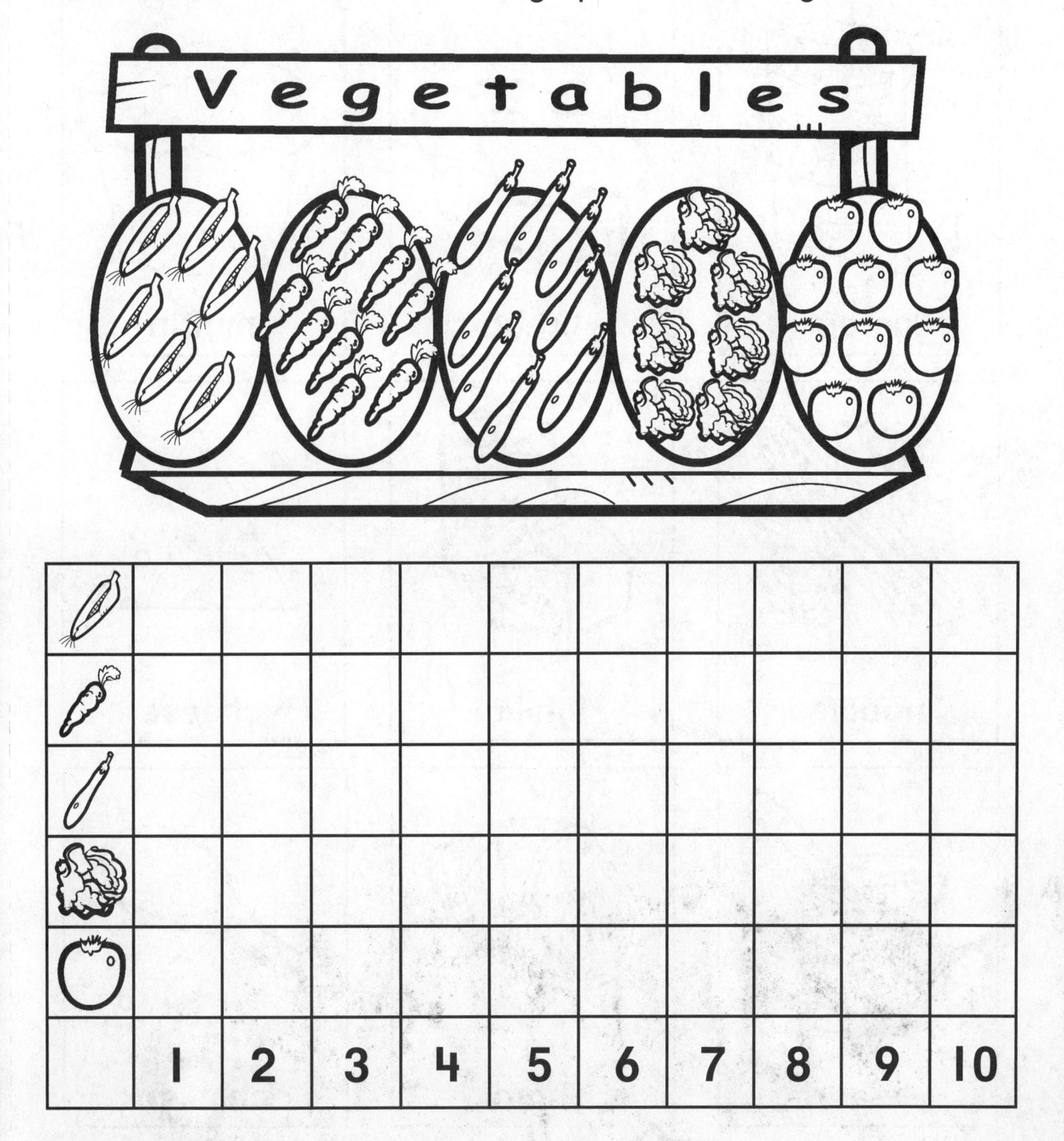

## Vegetables

| | 1 | 2 | 3 | 4 | 5 | 6 | 7 | 8 | 9 | 10 |

Use with "Graphic About Vegetables" on page 76.

# Food Picture Cards

Use with "Food Sort" on page 77.

| | | |
|---|---|---|
| **cereal** | **bread** | **muffin** |
| **noodles** | **milk** | **cheese** |
| **yogurt** | **ham** | **chicken** |

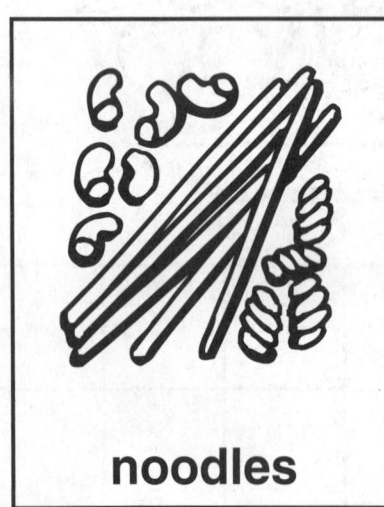

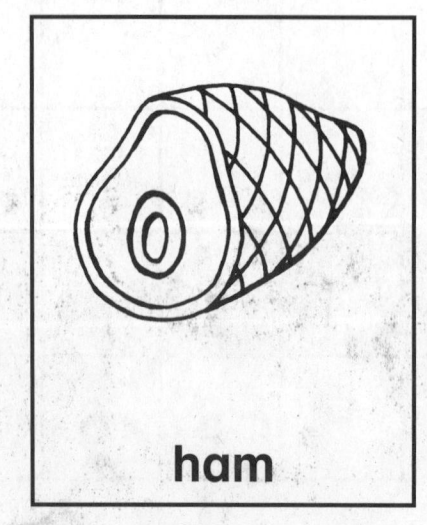

# Food Picture Cards

Use with "Food Sort" on page 77.

| nuts | beans | carrot |
| --- | --- | --- |
| squash | broccoli | apple |
| orange | banana | cake |

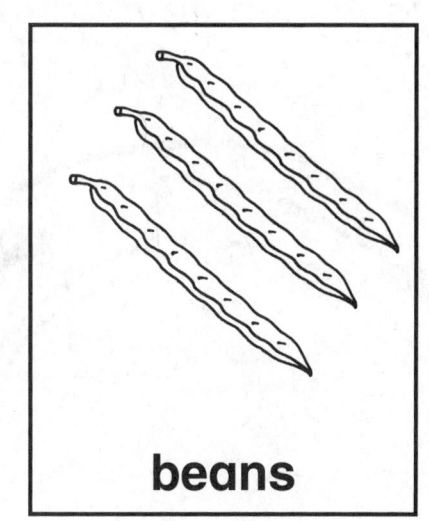

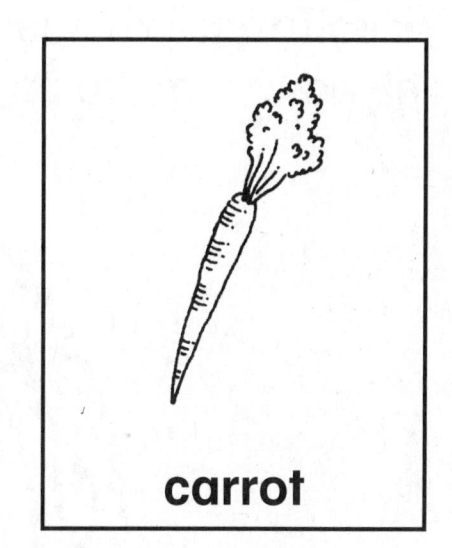

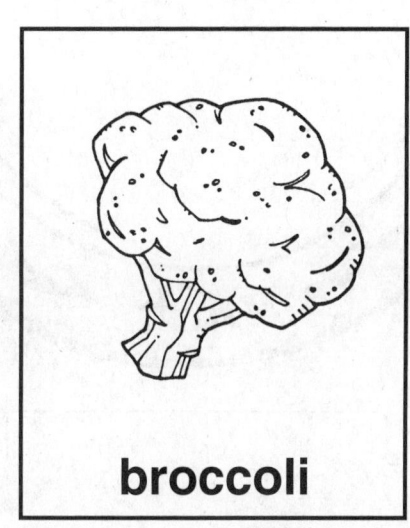

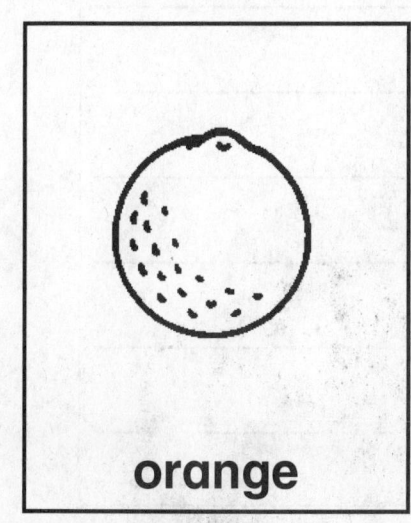

Name _____  Date _____

# My Favorite Food

**Directions:** What is your favorite food? Draw a picture of it. Tell how to make it.

Use with "Recipe Writing" on page 78.

Name _____ Date _____

# The Path to Good Health

**Directions:** Help the boy find the restaurant. Draw a line to show the way.

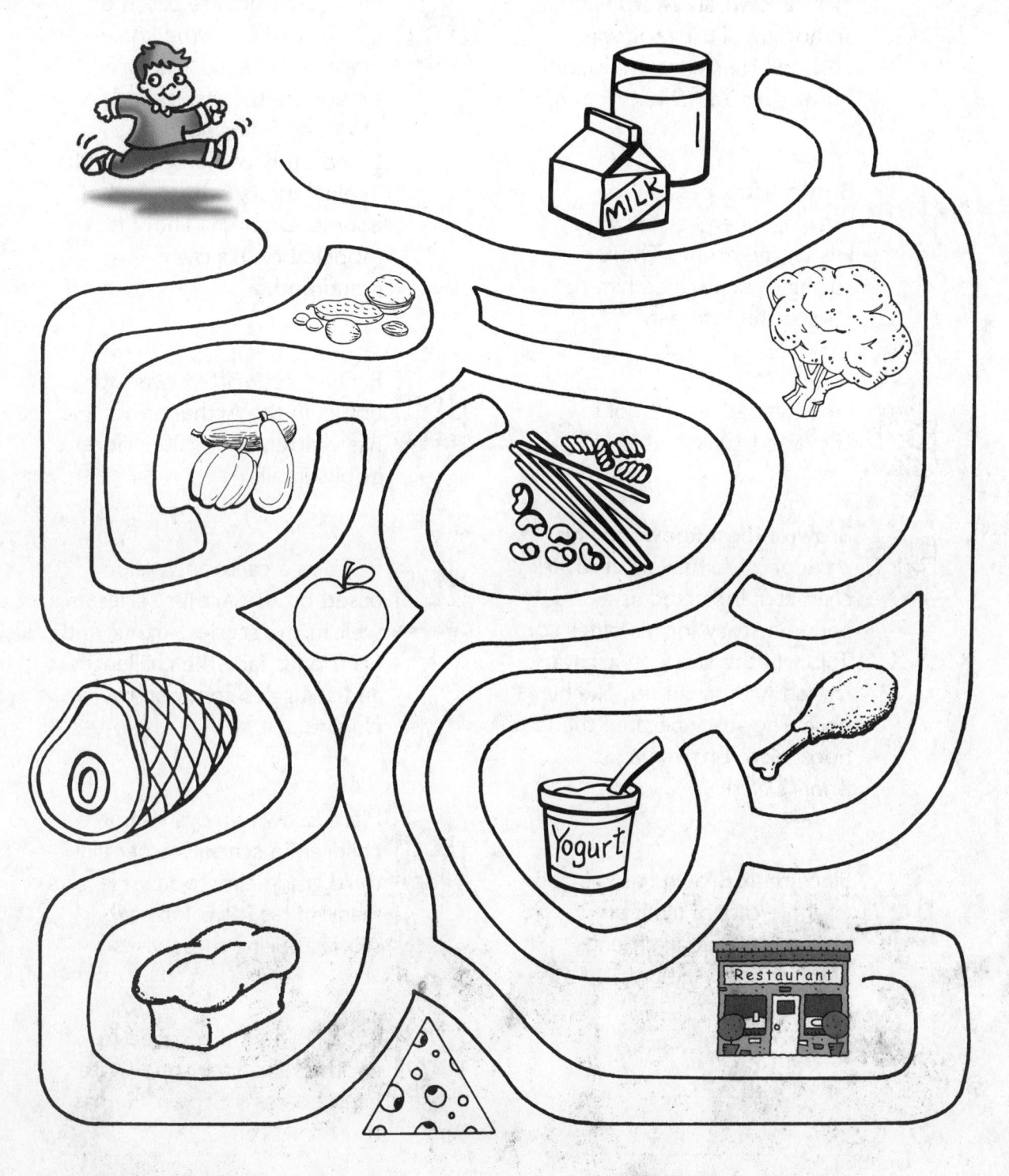

Use with "A-Maze-ing Food" on page 79.

www.harcourtschoolsupply.com
© Harcourt Achieve Inc. All rights reserved.

85

Unit 6, Food and You: Activity Master
Three Cheers for November 1–2, SV 9838-8

# A Look at Marc Brown

- Marc Brown, an award winning author and illustrator, was born in Erie, Pennsylvania, on November 25, 1946.

- Brown had a passion for drawing when he was young. His Grandmother Thora strongly encouraged him to pursue this interest.

- He attended art school in Cleveland, Ohio.

- Brown is best known for his creation of Arthur, an aardvark character. It started as a bedtime story for his older son, Tolon. In the story, an aardvark named Arthur did not like his nose. The story became the first book Marc Brown wrote, *Arthur's Nose*.

- Since then, Brown has created a whole cast of familiar characters that are friends and family to Arthur.

- His characters are based on friends and family he knew while growing up. His three sisters are the inspiration for D.W. and Francine. Buster is based on Brown's best friend in elementary school. And of course, Grandma Thora is modeled on his own grandmother.

- Brown has written over 30 books in the Arthur series. He has written over 100 children's books in all.

- PBS airs a cartoon version based on the Arthur series as well. In the stories, Arthur and his friends face the challenges and struggles common to children.

- Marc Brown enjoys visiting children in schools, especially third grade classrooms. He gets many of his ideas for new stories during these visits.

- Today Brown is married to another illustrator and writer, Laurie Krasny Brown. He has three children.

# Literature Selection: Arthur's Thanksgiving by Marc Brown

## Turkey Me

### Materials
- activity master on page 90
- crayons

### Directions

**Teacher Preparation:** Duplicate the activity master for each child.

Remind children that Arthur's friends and family dressed as turkeys at the end of the story to help Arthur. Then invite children to draw a picture of what they would look like if they were going to be the turkey in the play.

---

## Write a Play

### Materials
- activity master on page 91

### Directions

**Teacher Preparation:** Duplicate several activity masters for each child.

Group children and ask them to choose their favorite part of *Arthur's Thanksgiving*. Ask them to write the scene as a play. Show children how to write using a play format. Finally, have children present their play.

# Books by Marc Brown

- *Arthur Accused!* (Little, Brown & Company)
- *Arthur and the Crunch Cereal Contest* (Little, Brown & Company)
  (A book that can be used with the Food and You unit.)
- *Arthur Meets the President* (Joy Street)
  (A book that can be used with the Take a Vote unit.)
- *Arthur on the Farm* (Random House)
  (A book that can be used with the Magnificent Mammals unit.)
- *Arthur's Birthday* (Joy Street)
- *Arthur's Computer Disaster* (Little, Brown & Company)
- *Arthur's New Puppy* (Little, Brown & Company)
  (A book that can be used with the Magnificent Mammals unit.)
- *Arthur's Pet Business* (Joy Street)
  (A book that can be used with the Magnificent Mammals unit.)
- *Arthur's Reading Race* (Random House)
- *Arthur's Really Helpful Word Book* (Random House)
- *Arthur's Teacher Moves In* (Little, Brown & Company)
- *Arthur's Teacher Trouble* (Little Brown & Company)
- *Arthur's Tooth* (Joy Street)
- *Arthur's TV Trouble* (Little, Brown & Company)
- *Arthur's Underwear* (Little Brown & Company)
- *Bionic Bunny Show* (Little, Brown & Company)
- *Dinosaur's Divorce* (Little, Brown & Company)
- *D.W., the Picky Eater* (Little, Brown & Company)
  (A book that can be used with the Food and You unit.)
- *Glasses for D.W.* (Random House)
- *Where's Arthur's Gerbil?* (Random House)
  (A book that can be used with the Magnificent Mammals unit.)

# Bookmark Patterns

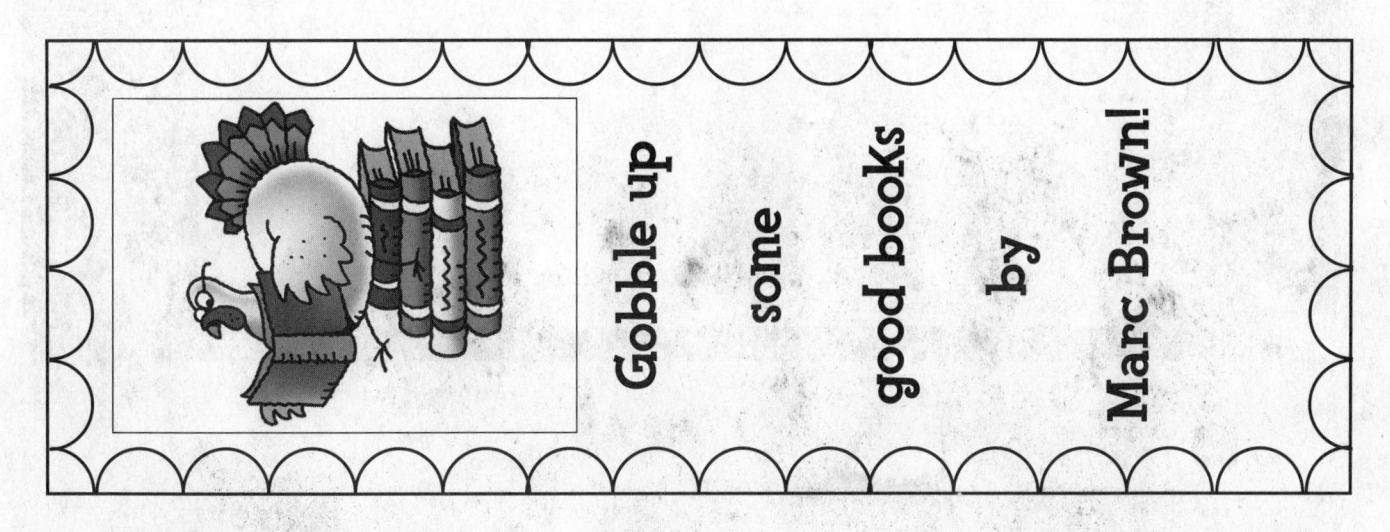

We are thankful for Marc Brown books!

Arthur is our favorite aardvark!

Gobble up some good books by Marc Brown!

Name _____ Date _____

# Play a Turkey

**Directions:** What would you look like if you were the turkey in Arthur's play? Draw a picture.

Use with "Turkey Me" on page 87.

Name _____   Date _____

# Arthur's Play

**Directions:** Work with some friends. What is your favorite part of *Arthur's Thanksgiving*? Write it as a play.

## Playbill

_____
_____
_____
_____
_____
_____
_____
_____
_____
_____

Use with "Write a Play" on page 87.

# Center Icons Patterns

**Art Center**

**Communication Center**

**Game Center**

**Language Center**

# Center Icons Patterns

**Literacy Center**

**Math Center**

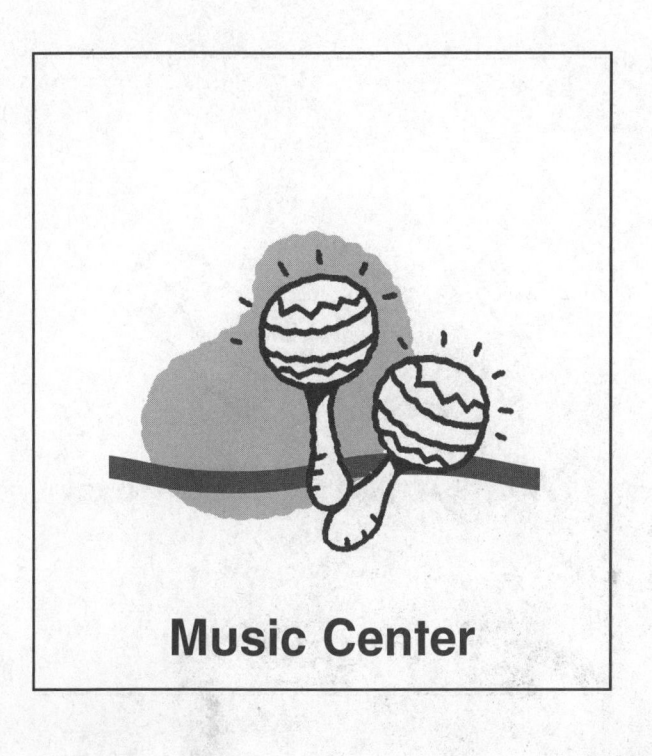

**Music Center**

**Physical Development Skills Center**

# Center Icons Patterns

**Science Center**

**Social Studies Center**

**Technology Center**

**Writing Center**

www.harcourtschoolsupply.com
© Harcourt Achieve Inc. All rights reserved.

**Center Icons Patterns**
Three Cheers for November 1–2, SV 9838-8

# Student Awards

You're doing a "beary" good job in

_____ ,
Child's name

_____
Teacher's signature

_____
Date

Congratulations, _____
Child's name

You are the November Student of the Month for

_____ .

_____
Teacher's signature

_____
Date

www.harcourtschoolsupply.com
© Harcourt Achieve Inc. All rights reserved.

**95**

Student Awards Patterns
Three Cheers for November 1–2, SV 9838-8

# Student Award

## Let's Celebrate!

_____
Child's name

can _____.

_____      _____
Teacher's signature                       Date

# Calendar Day Pattern

**Suggested Uses**
- Reproduce the card for each day of the month. Write the numerals on each card and place it on your class calendar. Use cards to mark special days.
- Reproduce to make cards to use in word ladders or word walls.
- Reproduce to make cards and write letters on each card. Children use the cards to play word games forming words.
- Reproduce to make cards to create matching or concentration games for children to use in activity centers. Choose from the following possible matching skills or create your own:
    — uppercase and lowercase letters
    — pictures of objects whose names rhyme, have the same beginning or ending sounds, or contain short or long vowels
    — pictures of adult animals and baby animals
    — number words and numerals
    — numerals and pictures of objects
    — colors and shapes
    — high-frequency sight words